WARNING

Anyone walking, scrambling, climbing, swimming or otherwise exploring Sark does so entirely at their own risk.

Individuals must assess each situation for themselves.

The Author cannot accept any responsibility for anything that may happen to a person or persons arising from this book.

Front Cover: In Derrible at High Tide
Back Cover: Derrible Headland seen over The Pot

This guide is in memory of my father
John Saumarez La Trobe Bateman
1905-1996
now buried in the Island church cemetery
and who introduced the family to Sark's coast and caves.

This guide is dedicated to my daughter
Alice

Thank you to the family (siblings and friends) who *inter alia* have come scrambling and caving over the years, assisted in the measuring, drafted some of the plans, proof read, provided and edited some photographs, and given encouragement for me to [eventually] publish.

Richard, James, Jeremy and Joly LTB, Mark and Tony G-B,
Tony Branson, Philip E-K, Pippa Blake, George Guille
...and Martina LTB for photographs including the front and back cover.

And finally, to remember our long suffering mother,
Mary La Trobe Bateman, who actively joined in our exploits

SARK

COAST AND CAVES

By

John F La Trobe Bateman

John F La Trobe Bateman
26 July 2018

WARNING

Anyone walking, scrambling, climbing, swimming or otherwise exploring Sark does so entirely at their own risk.

Individuals must assess each situation for themselves.

The Author cannot accept any responsibility for anything that may happen to a person or persons arising from this guide.

Beware of being cut off by a rising tide. All of Sark's bays have places where you can be cut off by a rising tide. Some of the scrambles described take a surprisingly long time, especially if you are looking into all the caves along the way: you should start any scrambles well before low water!

Sark Coast and Caves

by

John F La Trobe Bateman

First DRAFT edition titled "SARK COAST and CAVES" December 1988.

Second draft "A Measure of Sark Caves" (Family Edition) January 1998 and addendum 2002.

This "Sark Coast and Caves" edition 2012

Published by:
Maravilla Publishing
http://www.MaravillaPublishing.com

ISBN 978-0-9552409-3-5

Contents

Introduction

This book set out primarily to be about the Island's caves and low tide scrambles, and does not aspire to be a complete guide to Sark. However, a section at the beginning describes some of the footpaths and ways down to the sea.

Many of the caves described can only be reached on unusually low spring tides and so may not be accessible unless your visit was planned around a tide table. However, the Boutiques caves with the longest run underground can be accessed on any low tide, and the Dixcart Bay cave (the second longest around the Island) can be reached on any spring tide.

It has been compiled over several decades and the author hopes the reader will bear with the different styles of drawings. Be aware that the drawings are not all to the same or even a consistent set of scales! The coast and particularly the access from the land changes all the time.

Notes and Terms

Height of Tide

The level to which the tide will drop is a key factor when exploring the coast line of Sark. The tide levels given in this guide are referenced to "Chart Datum". A height given in this guide as CD+2.5m means a water level that is two and a half metres above chart datum, and these are the water levels given in the tide tables. Bear in mind that atmospheric pressure, wind and sea state will also affect the height of sea level. The height of tide is referenced to the Guernsey tide tables, but Sark's range and timing is very similar.

Spring and Neap Tides, and Times

The range of the tides is related to the phase of the moon. The largest range in a particular sequence normally being three tides after the full or new moon. Not all spring tides have the same range and an exceptional spring is needed to enter a number of the caves or negotiate some of the scrambles described here. There are typically spring tides with a larger than usual range around the equinoxes, but big springs occur at other times. Low water springs (LWS) occur in the early afternoon. Conversely, neap tides, with typically half the rise and fall of spring tides, occur around the first and last quarter of the moon: and high water neaps is in the middle of the day.

The time of the tides in the Channel Islands is roughly five hours before the time at Dover (or Southampton) However, if you are planning a holiday with the intention of exploring parts of the coast where access is restricted except on exceptional tides, you will need to consult a Guernsey tide table first.

Measurements

The cave lengths are all given in old fashioned feet (') and some of the widths in inches ("). Some measurements are even given in yards (yds) – 1 yard = 3' = 0.9144m. These are the units that the author was using when the first drawings were made! A simple conversion table is given at the back, see page 76.

Essential Equipment?

Footwear that can be worn whilst wading ... and a torch each.

"Low Tide Scramble"

This refers to negotiating a length of the coast line below the high tide mark and above sea level. You are no longer "low tide scrambling" if you have ventured above the high tide mark. Whilst you can wade and still be "scrambling", to the purist you are no longer "scrambling" if you are having to swim. A point about not scrambling above the high tide mark is that the surface is often unsafe.

This means that some sections of Sark's coast cannot be reached by a "pure" low tide scramble!

The classic low tide scrambles are "The Seven Caves", Les Fontaines (Little Sark) to Grande Grêve and "The Seven Dimples", but there are others.

Climbing?

Climbing around the coast of Sark above the high water mark is particularly dangerous: any surface above the high water mark is likely to be loose especially on the East coast. Below the high tide mark, the rocks are likely to be slippery so take care when "scrambling".

"Coasteering"

This is a new-to-the-author sport of scrambling around the coast in a wet suite. This has the advantage that sections of a scramble can be undertaken by wading or swimming. This makes for faster progress, and provides a safer way of reaching many of the caves.

Côtil

Côtil {pronounced co-ti} (pl Côtilles) is the non-arable land leading down to the sea.

Creux

This is a feature where there are one or more horizontal entrances at sea level with an opening to the land above. The largest and best known around Sark is the Derrible Creux. Others are the Creux Belêt, the Pot and a cave under the lighthouse. Some features are named "creux" when they do not, or no longer have, an opening above such as the Grand Creux and the Creux Noir et Blanc.

Flats

Areas of flat(ish) rock not necessarily level near the sea generally suitable for picnics or sunbathing.

Pignon

A "pignon" is a [historic] landing place to which there is a right of way from the top of the Island. Examples are the Pignon Rouge Terrier and the Pignon Port Gorey.

Souffleur

A cave where wave action compresses air inside causing a plume of spray outside.

G&L Latrobe Guide

The original Guide to Sark was by G&L Latrobe first published in 1913. This was revised by B.S. Allen in 1964. G&L Latrobe are understood to have visited the Island in 1911, 12 and 13: the third year it rained, so they wrote their guide. They were, in places, somewhat optimistic about the depth of some wades or they had very long legs!

Places and Caves (maplet)

Bec du Nez

Courbee du Nez

La Grune

Boutiques

Le Platon

green cave

New Place

Saignie

Port du Moulin

Pegane

Port a la Jument

Moie du Mouton

Home of the Gull

Gouliots

Saut a Juan

Brecqhou

Congriere

Landing

Fairy Arch

Fern Cave

Creux Belet

Red Cave (Drinking Horse Cave)

Grand Creux

Huitriere Cave

Blanc (Banquette) caves

Banquette

Greve de la Ville

Seven Caves

Lighthouse Creux

Dog Cave

La Valette

Maseline Caves

Big Sark

Harbours

Harve Gosselin and Fregondee

Victor Hugo

souffleur

Orgeries flats and caves

Port es Saies

Dixcart Bay Cave

The Crypt

Cathedral Cave

Brown Cave

The Dungeon

Derrible Headland

Derrible Headland East Caves

Derrible Headland Cave

La Grande Greve

Dixcart Bay

Noir Bais

Dixcart Souffleur

low red cave

Pigeon Cave

Canvanche Chasm and Caves

Lamentation Caves

Hogs Back Cave

Derrible Bay

Vermandaye fat man's misery

Creux Noir et Blanc

Les Fontaines

Little Sark

Moie Fano

The Pot

Sweet Pea Cave

Rouge Terrier

Moie de Breniere

Adonis Headland

Rouge Cane

Port Gorey

Louge Creek

Clouet Bay Caves

Venus Pool

Plat Rue Souffleur

L'Etac

Ways round and down to the sea

The way around Sark is generally on the "roads": this guide assumes that the reader has some knowledge of Sark and a reasonable map. However, there are interesting footpaths for those exploring the coast.

This section describes ways down to the sea. There are other routes down, but they are too dangerous to list! In this guide, some are categorised "easy', "moderate" and difficult". Sark is essentially a plateau 300' above the sea, so going down to the sea anywhere (and coming up again) requires a degree of fitness. Care is always necessary and you are responsible for your own safety. In recent decades, warning signs have appeared at some spots but the absence of a sign does not mean it is safe!

"easy": These ways down have a clear path (which may be steep) and steps, (possibly steep and not necessarily well defined). Any rocky parts will be [relatively] easy to negotiate. As everywhere around Sark's coast, some caution is necessary.

"moderate": The route has a path or reasonably identifiable sheep track, but may require a scramble down or over rack slabs or boulders to reach the bottom. Likely to require a head for heights and extra caution.

"difficult": steep, possibly dense undergrowth and/or a hint of scree, poorly defined route, heady and potentially dangerous.

Eperquerie Common

There are paths and "sheep tracks" all over the common. The key is a track which becomes a path along the spine of the Eperquerie. This leads eventually past the butts from the old musket practice range to the north end. To the east is the track to the Landing, the path to the top of Les Fontaines and the Creux Belêt, and a way down to the Congriere. To the west are ways down the Camel's Hump, to Le Platon and to the southern entrance to the Boutiques.

Eperquerie Common, north end

The half round tower by the butts is where the person putting up the targets on the butts would shelter: hopefully ricochets were not a problem. Drilled holes can be seen in the top of the rocks forming the butts.

The path along the spine of the Eperquerie peters out beyond the butts, but there is an obvious route on down towards the north end. There are a few steps to aid a final decent to sea level on east side of the end. Carrying on around the end towards the west (with the Pertu, the gap between Sark and La Grune on your right) and descending as you go leads round to the creeks that give access to the northern entrance to the Boutiques caves.

At low tide, you may scramble over or round La Grune and Le Corbée du Nez to Le Bec du Nez. There is a navigation light on Le Corbée du Nez.

Le Platon and Camel's Hump

Paths and tracks run round the West side of the Eperquerie. Starting from the end of the road at the South end of the common, a path runs west to above the Camel's Hump. It is possible to climb down to the sea here with care (*difficult*). Following on round along the top towards the gun above the landing, there is path down to Le Platon (*moderate*).

Congriere *(moderate)*

Start from the spine of the Eperquerie at the butts, and follow down the ridge to the East. This is a place for rod and line fishing.

Eperquerie Landing *(easy)*

Follow a well defined track almost to the sea. Easy access to the old landing beach, but a little scramble over some boulders to reach the man-made boating pool.

Eperquerie

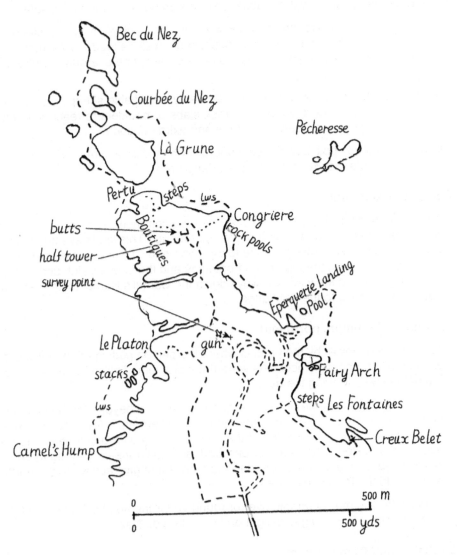

Les Fontaines *(easy)*

Paths (one starting half way down to the Eperquerie Landing) lead to the top of the bay. There is a short flight of concrete steps at the bottom.

Creux Belêt *(moderate)*

An extension of the path above Les Fontaines to the south leads above the Creux Belêt

Banquette *(easy - so far)*

A path from Le Fort leads down a valley to the Banquette, the final decent being over sloping rock (*"easy"* so far). The land above the Blanc Caves to the north is reached by battling through the undergrowth nearest to the sea.

Grêve de la Ville *(easy)*

Path all the way down with good steps at the bottom. The bay is the starting point for the "Seven Caves".

Valette *(difficult)*

The Valette (named after the Tenement at the top) is an inlet which can be reached from the extension to the north of the path from the Harbour Hill above the Maseline. Realistically, the Valette can only be reached in the spring before the undergrowth thickens up.

Harbours *(easy)*

Road all the way...with steps, a ramp or shingle to the sea!

Above the Maseline *(easy)*

A path starts a short way up the Harbour Hill on the right. It zig zags up steeply, and crosses over a spur, then down some, running above the back of the Maseline harbour and bay. The path eventually leads to a gate giving access to the side of a long field and a road between the power stations and the Mermaid. There is a dead end extension to this path continuing past the gate leading to the top south side of the little valley leading to the Valette.

Above the Creux Harbour *(easy)*

Starting on the left hand side of the Harbour Hill just above the low concrete water tanks, this leaves the path up the Harbour Hill and climbs up to a point overlooking the Creux Harbour, and incidentally with a vertical drop in front. This path continues up passing some sheds and the bottom of the field leading to the top of the way down Les Laches. This way becomes a track and then a road. There is a view point by a small aerial mast to the East: the narrow and steep ridge giving access to the Brown Cave *(difficult and dangerous)* is the next to the south. Meanwhile, this route passes the end of the field leading to Derrible

Les Laches *(moderate)*

Old path, ill defined in places and scramble at the bottom. This path is used by the fishermen to access their mooring lines and also gives access to the sea and the Cathedral caves.

Brown Cave *(difficult)*

See "Above the Creux Harbour" above. There is a little valley below the Sark effluent plant and the ridge down to the Brown Cave is on the left of this. There is no path or track but there is no other even remotely obvious or possible route down! The undergrowth at the top is fierce. Follow the ridge down: this is steep and requires considerable care not to slip.

Derrible ways

The starting place for access to Derrible is the dew pond, empty in recent years. At the high point to the east is one the six coast-wise map survey points. Looking towards the sea, the track to the left leads to Derrible bay and headland. To the right is a path to the Hog's Back.

Derrible Headland (difficult and especially dangerous)

Very difficult (and dangerous) unless reached by scrambling and swimming from Derrible Bay. See page 34 for a more detailed description.

Derrible Bay (easy ... a far as the flats at the bottom of the steps)

There is a path with approximately 175 steps down to flats, after which there are some slippery concrete steps leading to a boulder field.

Dew Pond to the Hog's Back (easy)

The path from the dew pond to the Hog's Back descends a series of steps passing through a small gate. At the bottom is, or was, a turning to the left leading to the top of the Derrible Creux: the Island no longer maintains this path on "health and safety" grounds, but the route can still be made out. Straight on, the path climbs up, winding some in amongst some low trees towards the top where the path along the spine of the Hog's Back is joined.

One way leads to the end of the Hog's Back and the other towards the village or on to Dixcart. To find this path from the village end, follow the road south from the Collinette (the crossroads by the Banks at the top of the Harbour Hill), continuing left at the first bend and right after a hundred yards or so at the Peingeurie. Follow this track between buildings and down to a gate in front leading to the Petit Dixcart. The path on the right here leads eventually to Dixcart (see next section). Left here passes up the side of a field, right along the top of a field and then becomes a path with tall [hawthorn] bushes on both sides. The path to the Derrible Dew Pond will be found a short way along on the left as the view along the top of the Hog's Back opens up.

The path along the top of the Hog's Back has views into both Derrible and Dixcart bays and south to Little Sark and L'Etac. The high point has an allegedly old fortified position and a cannon.

End of the Hog's Back (moderate/difficult)

The more intrepid can continue straight on down over the end to some flats or slightly to the right to reach the entrance to the Hog's Back cave. Over the end of the Hog's Back, there is no particular path or track, but ways can be found down to the flats. The final decent in to the creek leading to the west entrance to the Cave requires a little climb.

Here, as anywhere around Sark, be aware of currents if swimming off or near the end of headlands.

Roads, Tracks, Paths and ways down, Harbours to La Coupée

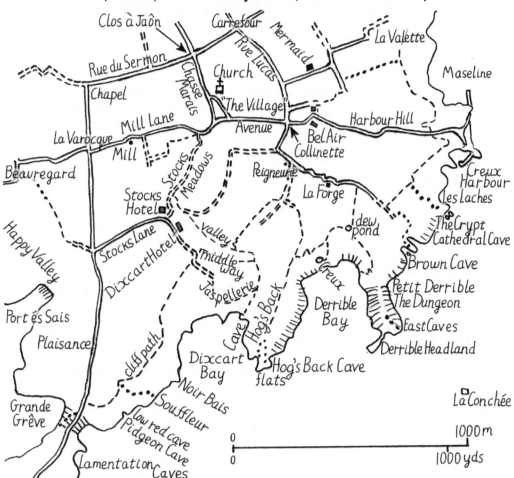

Paths to Dixcart Bay *(easy)*

These are the easiest ways down to any bay around Sark.

There are a number of ways to start down to Dixcart Bay, from the village via the **Peigneurie**, the **Valley**, the **Middle Way** and the **Jaspellerie** path.

From the Petit Dixcart gate mentioned above, a path to the right leads above the Petit Dixcart, drops down and joins the Valley path. The Valley path really starts at the Manoir: head down the track towards Stocks, bearing left before the hotel. Near the top of the wooded Dixcart (or Bakers) valley, the way is joined by a track from D'Icart (and the Pomme de Chien camp site). This path follows above the stream down the valley, and is joined at the side of Petit Dixcart by the path from the Peigneurie. The path continues down, crossing the stream and is joined in succession by the Middle Way and the Jaspellerie path. The vista opens up for the final stretch to the bay.

The Middle way starts from past the Dixcart Hotel. Where the track turns to the right beyond the hotel and Dixcart Cottage, there is a path to the left. The Middle way runs fairly straight down the west side of the Dixcart Valley.

11

Following the track past Dixcart Hotel and past the right hand turn in the track, there is a stile which is at the beginning of the "cliff path to La Coupée". The track on the left here leads to a path past the side of La Jaspellerie and round the top of Dixcart Bay with good views on the way down.

Cliff path to La Coupée *(easy)*

Climb over the stile mentioned above, continue up the side of the field, over another stile at the top and follow the path with bushes (sloe) on both sides. The path drops into a little valley, and up to views over Dixcart Bay and the Hog's Back, and then on towards Little Sark. There are a couple more dips before the path sweeps around the bottom of a field and arrives at La Coupée.

Dixcart Souffleur *(difficult)*

Access to the Dixcart Souffleur and hence to coast between the Noir Bais and the Pigeon Cave is by leaving the path to La Coupée after the last dip, see the Noir Bais to Pigeon Cave section, page 44.

La Coupée to The Mermaid *(easy)*

Following the paths described above in reverse order, you can walk almost all the way from La Coupée to the Mermaid without going on a road. From La Coupée, return along the cliff path to the stile near La Jaspellerie. Take either the Jaspellerie path or the Middle Way down into the Dixcart valley, up to the back of Petit Dixcart, and turn right, zig-zagging up onto the path towards the top gate for the Petit Dixcart. Continue on towards the Hog's Back, turning left onto the path to the Derrible dew pond.

Here you do need to walk along the side of the field back as if heading for the Village until you meet the road which is thankfully usually quiet here. Instead of turning left towards the village, turn right (towards the effluent plant) but taking a left before you get that far. This leads to the path above the Creux Harbour and eventually to the Harbour Hill near the bottom. You have to cross the Hill, and climb up the other side on the path above the Maseline...and hence almost to Mermaid or the Village.

Grand Grêve *(easy, care needed)*

The path starts at the north end of La Coupée and has many steps. The bottom part of the long standing path was covered by a rock slide, and a new [unofficial] path has been established further to the south.

The Pot *(moderate)*

Head south down the Little Sark road past the summit by the fort and down hill . At a gentle right in the road by Cider Press cottage, go left through the bank and follow the path which heads south once above the coast. The path leads eventually inside the pot itself. The final descent to the inside of the Pot, which is a creux, can be a little precarious and sometimes there is a length of rope to help.

Little Sark, Venus Pool and Port Gorey *(easy)*

Go down the Little Sark road, left at the Sablonnerie and left again after the well and before La Moserie. The track leads up, down across a dip and to a gate on the right sign posted to Venus Pool. Straight ahead is La Cloture (The Barracks) and a right of way leads round the property and down to Rouge Terrier.

Little Sark

La Grande Grêve

souffleur

La Pointe de la Joue

Lamentation Caves

Vermandaye Bay

Fort

La Baveuse

survey point

Moie Fano
(Puffin Headland)

Creux Noir et Blanc

Moie de la Fontaine

mill

Three Brothers

Les Fontaines

Adonis Headland

Duval

Sablonnerie

The Pot

Moie de
la Bretagne

Adonis Pool

engine house

Sweet Pea Cave

Rouge Câne

Pignon

chimneys

Rouge Terrier

Petit
Baveuse

Port Gorey

Moie de Breniere

Clouet

La Louge

Venus Pool

Moie de Port Gorey

souffleur

Platte Rue

Pierre du Cours

Sercule

Bretaigne Uset

0 ——————————— 1000m

0 ——————————— 1000yds

L'Etac

Through the gate and keeping left, two old silver mine ventilation chimneys can be seen. Follow the path to the right of these chimneys and down with thick brambles and bushes on either side. The path gives way into an open area: the start of the way down to Venus Pool is between two cairns (for more about Venus Pool, see page 50).

Back just through the gate, the path dropping down to the right leads down passed what remains of the old silver mine engine house (tower) to the side of Port Gorey where once upon a time there was a landing...for taking off the silver. On the left on the way down are the remains of other old silver mine buildings. The silver mines were ventilated by a tunnel from the valley to the chimneys at the top: a fire lit at the bottom created a draft up the tunnel which connected to a ventilation shaft from the mine to draw air up. Within living memory, it was possible to crawl inside this tunnel, starting just near the winding tower and emerging at the chimneys at the top, but this tunnel is believed to have since collapsed. Either way, it cannot now be considered safe.

To the left off this path on the way down, a path leads round above the Louge Creek, very close to the edge, eventually joining up with the more direct path to Venus Pool. To the right at the engine house is a path to the other side of Port Gorey.

Louge Creek *(moderate but need to push through undergrowth)*

The Louge Creek is a place for swimming and sunbathing and is to the east of Port Gorey. A way down leads to the west side of the creek running down the top of a spur. This starts from the coast path between Venus Pool and Port Gorey.

Port Gorey to Les Fontaines, Little Sark. *(easy)*

The path heading west from the engine house leads round above the west side of Port Gorey. There is a right of way down to a "pignon" on the west side of Port Gorey, but the path has not been maintained. Continuing along the top, the path little more than a sheep track in places leads round along the top of Rouge Câne to the headland above Adonis Pool and overlooking La Moie de la Bretaigne (Ship Rock). Further along, the way is less defined (but there are strategic stiles) and leads to the top of the path down Les Fontaines.

The path down Les Fontaines divides half way down. The left leads to the end of the creek, a good swimming place on the top half of the tide. The right leads down a path, needing a little more care due to part falling away, to the top of the creek.

There are ways down to Rouge Câne *(moderate)*, and over the end of Adonis Headland *(difficult)*, across a gully to Adonis Pool.

From the top of Les Fontaines, you find your way back to the road across the fields, keeping the Creux Noir et Blanc house to your north, passing round the back of the farm and onto the road at the back of La Pipeterie.

Top Stocks Lane to Beauregard *(easy)*

There is a track leading from opposite the top of Stocks Lane to the Beauregard. This passes beside the "Happy Valley" and now through a gate between a [new] vineyard and a bank. The Beauregard end of this route may change when a new hotel is built.

Moie des Orgeries *(difficult)*

The Orgeries are reached from the côtil behind the Beauregard. Although the way down is steep, the biggest problem tends to be finding a way through the prickles and thorns at the top. More details are on page 56.

Have Gosselin *(easy)* and Victor Hugo *(difficult)*

Starting from the Monument, there is an easy path down to the landing at Havre Gosselin. From here, you can make your way across the flats and creeks to the south but not as far as the entrance to the Victor Hugo cave.

To reach the flats beside the entrance to the Victor Hugo cave, start down towards Havre Goselin but continue straight on where the path turns right. Make your way down just to the right of the knolls through the undergrowth. You may pass some wire. Keep to your right of a gully on the sloping rock in the latter part of the descent. At the bottom, head to the left (south) to end up beside the entrance to the cave. The tide is never low enough to enter this cave dry.

Gouliot – Jument - Vaurocque

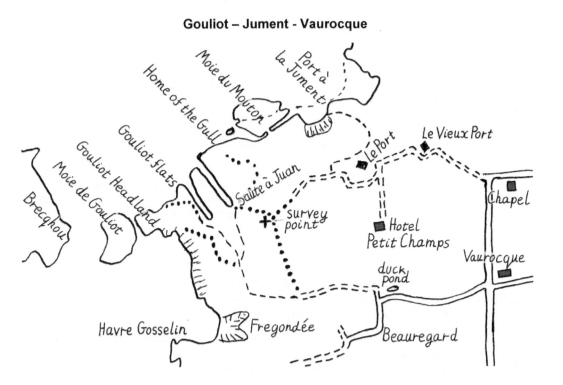

Gouliot Headland

Beyond the duck pond, right and immediately left, a track leads passed Beauchamp and through a gate to the côtil leading to the Gouliot headland. Straight on leads to various paths to the top of the Gouliot headland and ways down to the Gouliot caves *(moderate)*, the Gouliot Flats *(difficult)*, "Oven" *(easy)* and the "Island" *(difficult)*. There is a well defined route down to the caves, a right turn at the bottom of the dip before the headland proper.

Over the south side of the headland and a short way down is a flat area well sheltered and facing the sun known by some as the "Oven": and ideal spot for a picnic for those not enthused by climbing down. It is possible with considerable care to continue on down a scree like slope *(difficult, dangerous)* below the "Oven" keeping close to the side, cross a narrow slot (height of tide permitting) at the southern entrance to the Goiliot Inner Passage and arrive at "The Island". "The Island" has an area of gently sloping flats in front of the south side of the very end of the Gouliot Headland.

The spur immediately to the north of the Gouliot caves gives access to the Gouliot flats. Find you own way down exercising considerable care.

Turning right immediately through the gate onto the cotil above the Goulliot, you may follow uphill alongside a field bank until you reach a gap in the bank in front. One of the six survey points was here although there is nothing remaining to indicate such.

At the top of a pronounced little valley on the way to the headland, another path leads off to the north and round the top of, and dangerously close to, the Saut à Juan, a vertical drop into a creek. Just a little further on along the cotil, there is a way down below a [disused] quarry ("The Home of the Gull" – *difficult, thick undergrowth at the top*), but following up to the right leads to the survey point again.

Gouliot to Port à la Jument *(easy)*

Heading north from the survey point and keeping a field bank immediately on your left (west) leads down the side of a field and through a gate to a track. Around about the bottom of the hill along this track, on the left, will be found the beginning of the path down to Port à la Jument and the Moie du Mouton. The way historically used to go through Le Petit Port farm, and this new route leads round the back of the farm before the decent proper starts. Following the track again leads to the tractor and carriage route to the Petit Champ hotel and Le Port, eventually arriving at the corner by the Methodist chapel.

There is a picnic place overlooking the NW coast just off the track half way between the survey point and the top of the path to Port à la Jument. This is by a bend in the track and through a gap in the bank to an area that once may have been a small cultivated area.

Port du Moulin *(easy)*

The way down Port du Moulin begins just passed the Seigneurie and runs behind L'Ecluse. Staying straight on, the path is a dead end, but it runs around the top of Port du Moulin ending with a view over the Autelets and Seignie Bay.

The turning to the left just passed the back of L'Ecluse leads down a zig-zag, and then to a path leading down to the Window in the Rock. There are two paths to the left. The first leads to a recently cleared picnic and barbecue area. The second leads down over the stream, past a turning on the left onto Tintageu, and continuing curling down to Port du Moulin arriving on the shingle beach.

.....The following sections are about the coast and caves.

Bec to Les Fontaines

This stretch of coast past the Congriere is easy enough at low tide. There are some interesting rock pools nearer to the high water mark and a few short caves. The shore can be reached from East side of the Bec and from the Congriere. The Congriere is a place to go fishing and the rock pools are just to the south. In the middle of the inlet between the Congriere and Le Eperquerie landing is a cave about 50' long and plus or minus 4' wide: nothing special. Nearer Le Eperquerie landing, there is a cave about 35' long, very narrow and low about 15' from the back, but it widens out at the back. However, it is very stinky.

The Eperquerie landing is easily accessible down a wide track. Historically, this was the principle landing place, being one of the places where the beach is accessible to horses or wheeled vehicles from the top of the island. Here there is a man made pool which does not cover at neap tides: so the water will be fresher at springs!

The scramble from the Eperquerie landing south, possible at half tide, takes you through a short cave in line with the Fairy Arch, a small, but elegant rock arch at the North end of Les Fontaines bay. This is also a way through an archway nearer the land in the adjacent creek.

The path down to Les Fontaines (Big Sark) leaves the track where it first levels out and before a length of rail (ex WWII?) sticking up. This zig-zags down and there are some concrete steps for the final decent to the bay. An alternative path leaves the track down to the Eperquerie landing: at a steep left turn in the track about half way down, there is a right turning on to a path. This path runs quite low down across the top of Les Fontaines and on to Le Creux Belêt. There is a small cave, the Fern cave, at the back of Les Fontaines Bay. Le Creux Belêt is reached after a short scramble.

Fairy Arch, Eperquerie

Creux Belêt to La Grêve de La Ville

The deep creek into the coast south of the Huitriere drops from well above high water springs to well below LAT. Apart from this creek, the coast from the Creux Belêt to the Banquette is scrambleable.

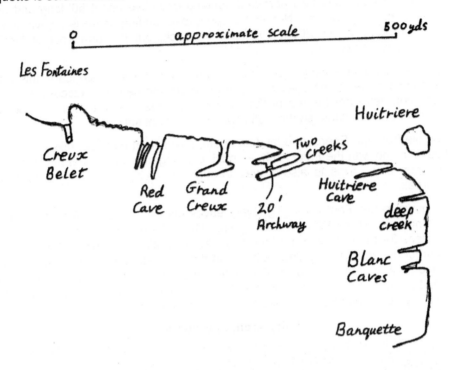

The path above the bay leads over the top of the top opening to this creux. Le Creux Belêt cave itself is about 55 feet long along the bottom and about 8 feet wide across the entrance.

Creux Belêt and beyond the Grand Creux

Heading East from Le Creux Belêt is a low tide scramble. The first caves are a pair, the first of which divides towards the back and is about 75 feet long. It has a double entrance with a pillar making a second entrance on the east side. The second cave is about 68 feet long.

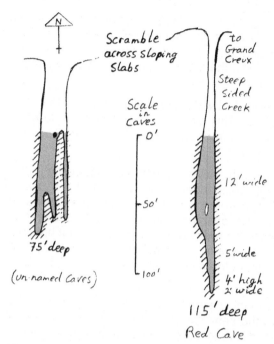

The next, quite red inside, is the Red Cave. This is about 115 feet long, and has a pillar dividing the cave about 50 feet in. This pillar looks like a drinking horse and this cave is also known as the Drinking Horse cave[1].

There are a couple of narrow caves opposite the Huitriere, on the corner where the coast turns from running to the East to South.

Huitriere Cave

The Huitriere Cave is low down amongst some small creeks on the corner opposite the Huitriere rock. The approach creek is long and almost covered over. Although the cave itself is only 95 feet long, it feels much more because it is so narrow!

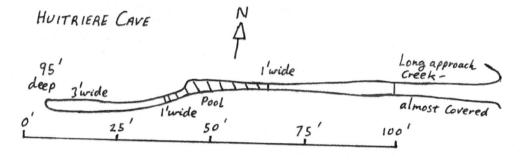

---

[1] G&L Latrobe. The B S Allen revision refers to one of the Blanc caves as the Drinking Horse cave.

Banquette or Blanc Caves

North of the Banquette are two small, but interesting caves. The entrance to the Northern most looks like a drinking horse at some tides, so this could also be the Drinking Horse cave. The caves are also named the Blanc Cave on one map[2].

These caves can be accessed from the path down to the Banquette. From the last bend, make round to the left walking just below the bracken. The Southern cave is in the first obvious creek. A low spring is required to enter the easy way from the end of the creek. It is possible to climb down the side of the creek close to the entrance - with care - and enter the cave dry on a CD+2.5m tide.

This cave is about twelve feet wide and high for the first forty or fifty feet, the longer part bearing round to the left. This left hand branch reduces to about two foot six wide and the end is about eighty feet from the entrance. It widens out a little before the end, and the roof is high all the way in.

The right hand branch of the cave is much more interesting. It runs straight in from the entrance along the right hand side, the larger part of the cave bearing away after forty feet. Ten feet in (fifty feet from the main entrance), the cave is very narrow, about fifteen inches wide, although it too opens out again to about three feet wide before the end. The ceiling also comes steadily lower towards the back, but it has the most magnificent, wide quartz veins with large crystals. It is hoped that enthusiasts of Sark caves who have reached this far will admire them where they are, and not try and chip chunks out to take away...

Leaving the entrance to this cave, it is a reasonably easy climb up over the left hand side of the creek towards the seaward end. Heading north across the slabs, a deep, very narrow crack is crossed and then down into the next creek which has a rock standing in its entrance.

There is another rock across the entrance to the cave which can be stooped under. The cave is about six feet wide at the entrance, and tapers down to about four feet in the first half of its total depth. At fifty feet in, the cave has narrowed to a fat man's misery, and is barely one foot wide at one point. However, it opens out to give comfortable standing room at the end, which is eighty eight feet from the entrance. There is a thin quartz vein along the side, but is a poor offering after that in the previous cave.

There is a way up to the north from the entrance to this cave. It is much the easiest climb up or down of all those encountered so far in accessing these two caves. Unfortunately, it leads into the bracken and worse, but it does offer an alternative route for those who are not confident climbers. Coming round from the Banquette, make up into the bracken just before the first creek. A dry stone wall will be crossed (beware of the ditch on the up side), and then strike across towards the lowest of a straggly line of (sycamore) trees. A short distance further along is an old dry stone wall running away from the sea which marks the point to strike down to north side of the caves.

---

[2] R.M. (Reg) Titford, 1978.

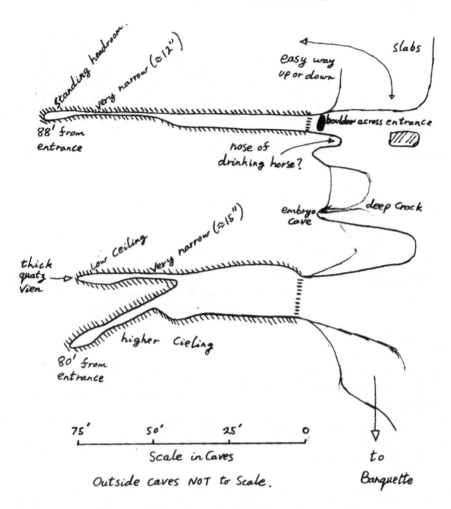

standing headroom.

very narrow (≈12")

slabs

easy way
up or down

88' from
entrance

boulder across entrance

nose of
drinking horse?

embryo
cave

deep crack

thick
quatz
vien

low ceiling

very narrow (≈15")

higher cieling

80' from
entrance

75'	50'	25'	0

Scale in Caves

Outside caves NOT to Scale.

to
Banquette

Banquette to La Grêve de la Ville

This is a rocky low tide scramble. The most noticeable feature of this coast is that this is where the tree line comes closest to the sea, and is interesting because this is quite different from anywhere else around the Island. Even where you can climb up from the coast line, you will find the undergrowth above impenetrable.

La Grêve de la Ville bay itself is shingle at high tide (good for morning swimming) and small round weed covered boulders at low tide. There is a natural arch towards the east of the bay before the Gulls Chapel and the start of the Seven Caves.

Seven Caves

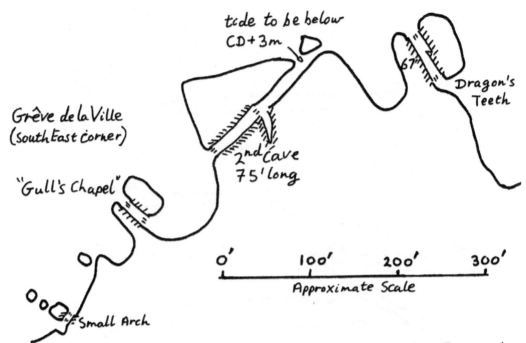

tide to be below CD+3m

Greve de la Ville (South East corner)

"Gull's Chapel"

2nd Cave 75' long

Dragon's Teeth

Small Arch

0'   100'   200'   300'

Approximate Scale

The "Seven Caves" is a low tide scramble that takes in a number of caves. Everyone has their own way of counting them. The scramble needs a tide below CD+2m. It is possible to extend the scramble to include the Dog Cave, but this requires a CD+0.5m tide.

The start is at the SW corner of La Grêve de la Ville. Whilst making for the Gulls Chapel which is the first cave, a small arch will be passed at the top of the beach. Its a sea-weedy, bouldery scramble up to and through the Chapel, as indeed are many other sections of the Seven Caves.

Once through the top end of the Gulls Chapel, make your way over to the left onto a relatively recent fall (1988) where the entrance to the second cave will be found. This cave runs steadily down hill for about seventy five feet and continues as a creek of the same width. There are spaces running off to the right of this cave near the bottom end, up to 38' long and one with a higher window opening. The bottom of this creek has a pool which can usually be crossed without getting your feet wet by judicious use of the ledges at the sides and an occasional, carefully placed rock.

The bottom of the creek is the first critical point with the tide which must be below CD+3m to round the point. At the far side of the little inlet is the entrance to the next cave. The way across and the way in are bouldery!

This cave starts off wide, but half way along, it narrows dramatically. You will have to climb up in a very narrow slot. Fortunately for the more substantially built, the slot widens as it goes up, so you can chimney up until it is sufficiently wide to proceed. This cave exists at the top of the tidal range through a low opening with dragons teeth projecting down from the top.

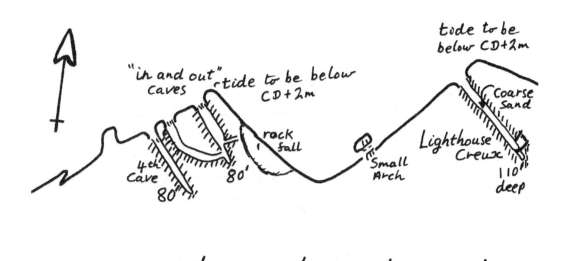

"in and out" caves   tide to be below CD+2m

tide to be below CD+2m

4th Cave   80'   rock fall   Small Arch   Lighthouse Creux   Coarse sand   110' deep

80'   80'

0'   100'   200'   300'
Approximate Scale

Exit through The Dragon's Teeth

Seven Caves, 4th and "In and Out" caves

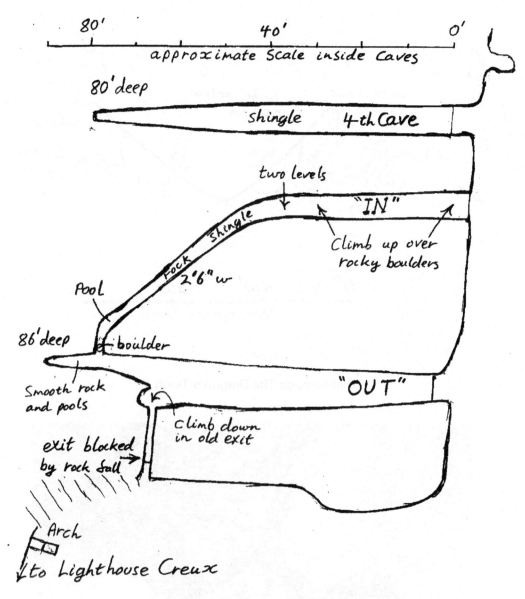

80'
40'
0'
approximate Scale inside Caves

80' deep
shingle
4th Cave

two levels
"IN"
Climb up over
rocky boulders

Rock Shingle
2'6"w
Pool

86' deep
boulder

"OUT"

Smooth rock
and pools

Climb down
in old exit

exit blocked
by rock fall

Arch
to Lighthouse Creux

From this exit, two points can be seen. The second is the end of the Seven Caves scramble as such. In front of the first point, there are three cave openings. The opening farthest from the sea is a straight, eighty foot long cave with a shingle bottom that tapers in width and height from entrance to the back. The other two caves meet at the back, although this is not readily apparent even from inside.

Enter the seaward cave. It is about ten feet wide, and towards the back the shingle bottom gives way to rock. The cave narrows and ends some eighty foot from the entrance. Easily missed, even carrying a torch, is an opening on the right about ten feet from the back although a draft should be felt as you pass. The opening is about two feet wide and six feet high and, after climbing over a boulder, about six feet long. It leads to a higher cave with a shingle bottom. This goes round a corner, the bottom giving way to rock again, and back outside through the middle entrance.

There is another exit from the seaward cave. At the point where the seaward arm narrows, there is another exit on the left. A rock fall in the 1990s has blocked the creek exit, but it is still possible to crawl into the cave section from inside the main cave.

The next point requires a CD+2m tide. Across this rocky bay is the Lighthouse Creux, but there is a small archway to look at against the cliff on the way. The Creux cave has a coarse sand and shingle bottom, and is between eight and four feet wide for most of its length. Just under a hundred feet in, there is the creux opening above. Light can be seen coming from a large entrance high up to the left and also from a smaller, even higher and ahead. There is also a small crack, about a foot wide, on the left side of the end of the cave which leads back another twelve feet.

This is the end of the Seven Caves, but it is possible to continue round the coast under the lighthouse to the Dog Cave. Like the last point, the one on the corner here requires a CD+2m tide. It is a long scramble over large rocks, and is generally easier higher up: at least the rocks have little seaweed on them. There is a thirty-foot long cave ("Matt's" cave) on the way round, with a comparatively wide opening and a narrow, twisted rear. The final point immediately before the Dog Cave requires a CD+0.5m tide.

Dog Cave and the "Tail of the Dog"

The Dog Cave is long, wide and high, with three long side caves on the right. The floor of the cave is shingle or coarse sand and is easy to walk along. The roof is particularly high towards the back by the beginning of the last side cave and in the middle side cave. These high, domed sections glisten in torchlight, presumably from salts carried through from the earth above.

The south side of the entrance to the Dog Cave has a vertical cliff face. The bottom is about one meter below chart datum: a wade through long, tough seaweed is always necessary to reach La Valette and the Maseline Bay.

The specialty of the Dog Cave is that about 120 feet in, opposite the middle of the right hand side caves, is a narrow crack on the left. Climbing along and up this crack eventually leads to a place with a bottom at about the high tide mark and a perceivable roof as well as sides. The roof of this part of the cave is progressively lower towards the back, but there is an exit through a small sump, up along a 45% slope about twenty five feet to an exit in a couloir between the Dog Cave entrance and the Valette.

The exit from the sump to the couloir is only just large enough to crawl up and is not through solid rock: expect to get muddy dirty. A helping hand at the exit makes life easier.

A word of warning: the author checked the exit to the couloir before trying to climb through the cave! As far as is known, this second exit from the Dog Cave was first found on 16 August 1989. This was a second survey of the cave, the first on 30 August 1988 totally failing to notice this crack! The first time anyone actually crawled all the way through this cave is believed to have been in August 1990 by John F and Richard LTB. This employed an expedition mounted from the sea, landing parties by boat to clear the sump at the bottom of the couloir entrance before attempting the cave from the main entrance.

The Dog Cave

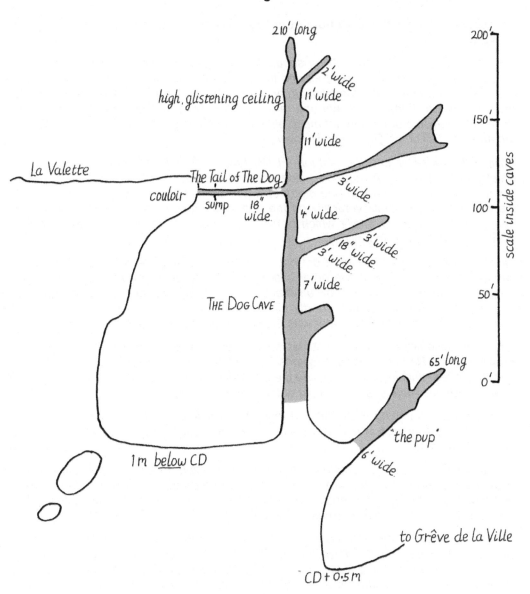

Up to Our Necks

An account of a low tide scramble from Gréve de la Ville to the Maseline Jetty, 16 August 1989.

Well, of course, low tide scrambling should incorporate careful calculation based on tide tables, local knowledge, the right kit and the best available guide book information. The intention was to start at the Maseline Jetty, survey the caves in the Maseline Bay, verify a previous sketch of the Dog Cave and return via the Seven Caves. In the event, it was done in the reverse order and not much else went according to plan. But we all had great fun and the "Tail of the Dog" was discovered.

Philip Edwardes-Ker and the Author(JFLTB) had confirmed the previous year that La Valette to the Dog Cave requires a tide one meter below chart datum: that is, you will always have to wade through one meter of water! In fact, the seaweed round the end is the sort with a thick stalk vertically off the bottom for about one meter and brown, flat, heavy fonds lying horizontally which is nigh on impossible to wade through. In other words, you have to swim anyway.

Since we would have to swim, it did not seem to matter that the tide would not be low enough to avoid wading at two other critical places, the seaward exit from the Cagnon Cave (entered by the phone box on the Maseline Jetty) and at the South end of the archway (a small gulls chapel) shortly afterwards. These points need the tide down to CD+0.25m: the predicted low water was CD+1.85m (16 August 1989).

The team assembled at the Bel Air at 10.30, Tony Branson, Mark and Chris Gordon-Brown, George Renoylds, Philip Edwards-Ker and JFLTB. A hint of things to come came with the coffee (drinking coffee outside the Bel Air was unusual for this lot in itself): JFLTB returned with six white in spite of most of the requests being for black.

Everyone was champing at the bit and ready to go before 11.00, but low water was not until 13.15, so a change of plan was made. We would start at the other end and "do" the Seven Caves first.

The Seven Caves were scrambled in true low tide fashion: the tide was just low enough at all the critical points climb around without getting the teams feet wet – that is except those who slipped into rock pools anyway. PE-K caught up after being delayed by a breakfast top up on the blackberries on the way down to La Gréve de la Ville.

Over the boulders at the South of Gréve de la Ville, up through the Gulls Chapel (one of several around the island), down through the Second Cave with a quick look into the "miseries" on the right hand side. Round and up through the Dragons Teeth, and across to the Fourth Cave and the "In and Out". After careful consideration, even the thinnest considered that the shingle was too high to be able to exit from the In and Out via the low side cave, although JFLTB and AFJLTB had been through it eight months before. The shingle was also very high at the back of the Lighthouse Cave, the last of the Seven Caves.

And so, the Seven Caves were more or less routine, and the team scrambled round under the lighthouse heading for the Dog Cave…and the first debacle.

JFLTB (Yellow Leader) was convinced that the a "wade" would be necessary at the last point before the Dog Cave. This "wade" rapidly degenerated into a "swim", backstroke carrying his pack. Vigorous kicking lost both of JFLTB's plastic sandals which were held out as being THE GEAR for scrambling, and which belonged to an absent younger brother! The water was too murky and weedy for any chance of recovery. The team *followed through, except for PE-K who was bringing up the rear and sneakily found a way of climbing over the top. And so the team arrived at the mouth of the Dog Cave, PE-K still dry and wearing a dry (red stripy) shirt.*

A detailed survey of the Dog Cave followed. This included the discovery of day light at the end of a side arm to the left. This side arm is entered via a tall but narrow crack, which has to be crawled through lying on your side. This eventually widens out sufficiently for you to be able to turn round.

Below the high tide mark, the back is just under 30 feet from the main cave. However, crawling to a higher level, above high water, daylight was visible at the back through an opening about one foot high and nine inches wide. The bottom was fine gravel and looked like it could be dug out[3].

The main part of the Dog Cave is just over 200 feet long. There are three arms to the right in addition to the crack on the left. The ceiling is high and glistens in the torch light at the highest places.

The Team outside the Maseline Halls

Chris   Mark   George   Tony   Philip   John

Everybody had to swim leaving the main entrance of the Dog Cave towards La Valette: everybody got wet and more or less every thing got damp – except PE-K's shirt, which somehow he kept dry all day.

In a couloir before La Valette bay, the probable entrance to the "Tail of the Dog" was found about twenty feet above the high water mark[4]. There is a fault in the rock at this point. Water obviously flows down this fault into this entrance: this would explain the loose gravel at the bottom of the back entrance to the Dog Cave.

---

[3] The expedition the following year dug out this gravel after entering this cave via the shaft from the outside.

[4] Confirmed the following year.

The scramble and climb from La Valette to the Maseline Caves was achieved without swimming, but did involve wading thigh deep and climbing half in and half out of the sea. The Maseline caves were duly surveyed and the team picture taken outside the Maseline Halls.

The water was by now deep through the Maseline Arch. George swam to a Frenchman passing in his dingy, and persuaded him to collect our bags and take them to the jetty. The team finished the scramble by swimming, JFLTB and Mark Gordon Brown making the very last section dry via the Cagnon Cave.

Thus ended a scramble that broke most of the conventions, with a section above the high tide mark and sections, frankly, below water!

Maseline Bay

The tide is never low enough to scramble from the Dog cave to the Maseline Bay without a swim. La Valette can be reached via the south side of the little valley from the very end of the footpath starting at the north side of the bottom of the harbor hill: however, this is very overgrown after the spring. At the very north of the Maseline Bay, north of La Valette, is the couloir into which leads the Tail of the Dog.

The Maseline Halls

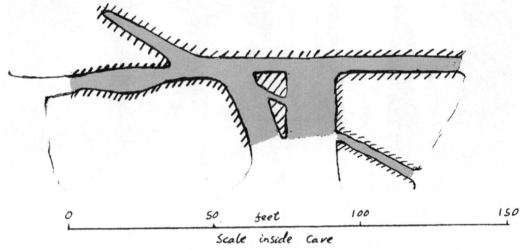

Scale inside Cave

The main cave system is the Maseline Halls at the back of the bay, and a CD+1.0m tide is required to reach it from La Valette. The main cave runs parallel with the coast with an entrance at both ends, and is about 135 feet long. This main cave has two seaward halls, and another cave running at an angle across them all and continuing as a separate cave to the North. In line with the main cave, but about 78 feet to the south, is another cave parallel to the coast and about 62 feet long. The southern entrance to this section of cave leads up over a rock fall into a large amphitheatre like opening, 50 feet wide and 20 feet deep, which is clearly visible from the Maseline Jetty.

The Maseline jetty is reached by way of the Gulls Chapel and the tractor turning area at the head of the harbor, a tide well below CD+1m being needed to negotiate the Southern entrance to the Gulls Chapel dry.

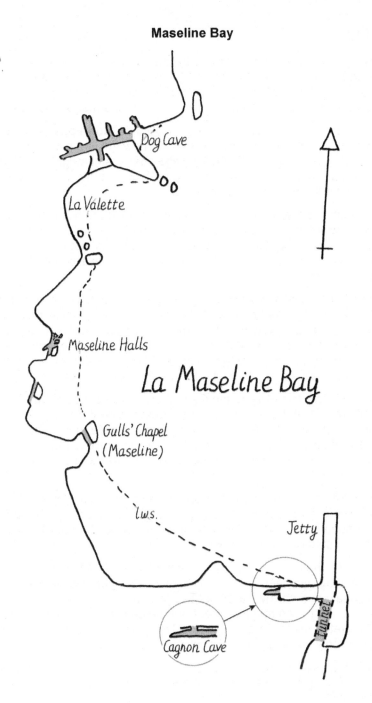

There used to be a cave, the Cagnon Cave, where the extended tractor turning area at the head of the harbour is now. The stub end of this cave can still be seen behind a mesh screen.

Cathedral Caves

There are two long caves just south of Les Laches creek. The second is the Cathedral Cave and the first, which had no name up 1988, is now known as "The Crypt" – logically being alongside the Cathedral and deeper   Both can be reached after a short, easy scramble on a CD+0.5m tide. The start is from the old fisherman's landing at Les Laches.

Take the road south from the crossroads at La Collinette, down passed La Forge and up passed the path off to Derrible. Before the Island's new effluent plant, the track turns left down hill again. At the gateway to some carriage sheds, strike right round the bottom of the field and the path down to the landing will be found on the left. The bottom of the path arrives at the north end of the Laches creek.

Head South through the creek, crossing the intersecting creek from the sea and passing Le Platon a Mole, which has a small archway through it. It may be necessary to splash through a pool. There is a stretch of seaweed covered rocks, but the entrance to the first cave (The Crypt) is just here on the left. Access to this cave should be possible on a CD+0.75m tide.

This cave is two hundred and seventy feet long, but narrow, often four or five feet wide, rarely more than eight. It does open out at the back however, where there is a chamber almost thirty feet in diameter, forty feet high and with a fifteen foot side arm on each side. The cave curves just enough towards the end so that the entrance cannot quite be seen from the back. There is a thigh deep pool just inside the entrance, which cannot be climbed over, and a shallower pool about three quarters of the way in.

The short scramble from this cave to the Cathedral Cave requires a CD+0.5m tide. This cave is quite different from the last one. Immediately inside the entrance, the main cave turns about thirty degrees to the left. Straight on, a lower cave runs in about fifty feet from the entrance, and then it too turns to the left. The end of this lower cave is just over seventy five feet from the entrance, and the last twenty five feet (from the turn) are only about two feet wide, with an eight foot ceiling.

Fifty foot from entrance, the main cave is obstructed by two large rocks whose top is at about CD+7m. There is easy passage on either side of the central rock on foot, but they effectively block boats from proceeding any further except at the top of springs. (There is room for a canoe to squeeze passed however).

One hundred feet in, the cave is about eight feet wide, and makes a thirty degree turn to the right. After another fifty feet, the cave widens out to about twelve feet wide, and then turns to the left again and narrows to about two feet wide. The back of the cave is at the end of this section, about two hundred feet from the entrance. It widens out to about five feet for a short stretch just before the back. The main cave is high all the way along, although the top is only visible up a narrow slot towards the back.

From the plan of the cave, it appears that the end section of the main cave is in line with the back section of the smaller cave straight ahead in the entrance. Have these sections struck the same fault?

Cathedral Caves

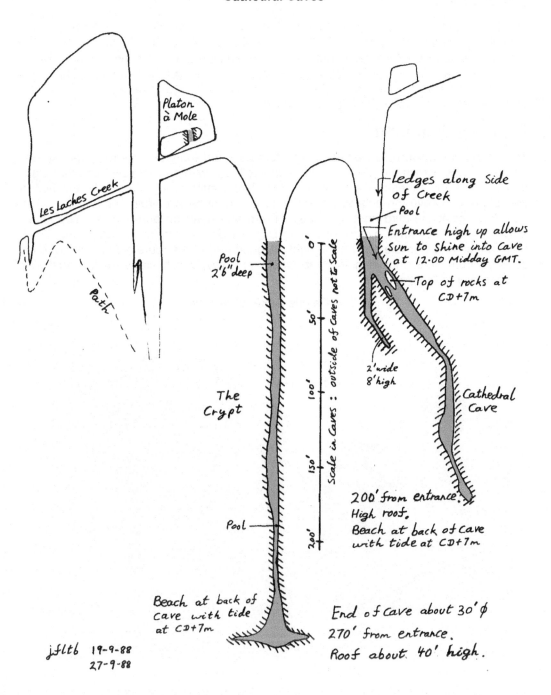

Platon à Mole

Les Laches Creek

Path

Pool 2'6" deep

The Crypt

Pool

Beach at back of Cave with tide at CD+7m

Scale in Caves : outside of Caves not to Scale

0'
50'
100'
150'
200'

Ledges along Side of Creek

Pool

Entrance high up allows Sun to Shine into Cave at 12.00 Midday GMT.

Top of rocks at CD+7m

2' wide 8' high

Cathedral Cave

200' from entrance. High roof. Beach at back of Cave with tide at CD+7m

End of Cave about 30' ⌀ 270' from entrance. Roof about 40' high.

jfltb 19-9-88
27-9-88

Brown Cave

The Brown Cave, between the Cathedral Cave and Petit Derrible, cannot be reached by scrambling. The way down from Sark, which is steep at times and not very safe, is from the South side of the little valley below the Sark effluent plant. Continue down towards the sea onto a little headland, and then down the slabs to the right (South). The Brown Cave at the back of the creek to the South and is about 115' wide and 15' wide. The cave is higher at the back than at the entrance.

Derrible Headland

The safest way to Derrible Headland is to scramble and swim around from Derrible Bay. There is a way across the "Devil's Dyke" but only those with an excellent head for heights and the sure footedness of a mountain goat should attempt it. Start down the path to Derrible Bay. Leave the path at either the second right hand hairpin turn and cut across and down or at the third right hand hairpin turn and head up and across. You should arrive at the lower knoll overlooking Petit Derrible on the left (to the east), the Devil's Dyke ahead and Derrible bay on the right. A good part of the route across the Dyke can be seen from here, including the gap where the way, which starts on the east side, crosses over to the west side.

The Devil's Dyke, East Side

Route onto Devil's Dyke

To the east of the knoll, over the left hand edge, there is a platform about three feet down. Climb down onto this platform and then down, initially away from the Dyke and then round under at a lower level. The last twenty feet to the gap in the Dyke is at the same height. There used to be a boulder filling this gap. Now that it has gone, it is a simple matter to walk through to the Bay side, and along a rock slab. Climb up the corner. The old pathway to the top round the east of a rock stack is still visible and just useable in the dry, but it does not feel very secure. It is easier to climb up a little further round the right of middle of the three stacks at this point on the headland.

This part of the headland has a definite back-bone and the SSE end of the top is a good point from which to view the next steps. There are ways down to the Derrible Headland East caves and to the right (SW) from here down a ridge to a col leading to the rest of the headland.

The easiest way down to the east caves is to look towards La Conchee (the square rock off the end of the headland) and head down a little to the right of this line. Keeping clear of the top of the entrance to the cave on the left, a v-shaped rock gully will be found which gives easy access to the slabs below. The creek on the left has ledges along the side which allow the east entrance to the cave to be gained without getting wet with a three meter rise of tide (above Chart Datum).

Below the col leading to the end of the headland on the bay side is a rock flat suitable for swimming at high to half tide. On a low tide, the cave through the headland can be reached from a small, shingle beach here.

Between the col and the end of the headland, there are three humps. You can walk round the bay side of these, just above the bramble line, or climb over each rock hump. The point has a small rock bridge to the slab at the end. The rock is solid and makes for good climbing. But beware of the current if swimming anywhere off the end or east of Derrible Headland.

Outline of Derrible Headland

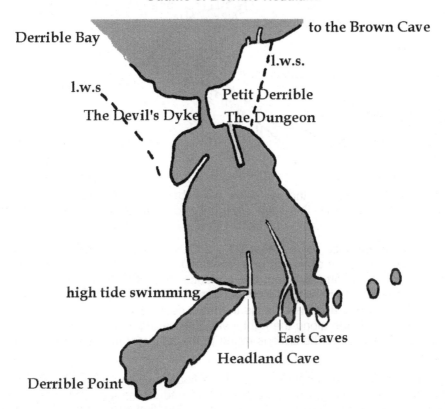

Derrible Headland Caves

These caves can be explored starting from either the west or east side of the headland. The west side can be reached from the col leading to the end of the headland as described above, or by scrambling round from Derrible Bay, a preferred approach for those unwilling to tackle the Devil's Dyke. The scramble round from Derrible Bay is easy. The critical point is to reach the sand beach in front of the creek. This needs a tide of CD+1.9m whether approached from the headland or from the bay.

Derrible Headland Cave

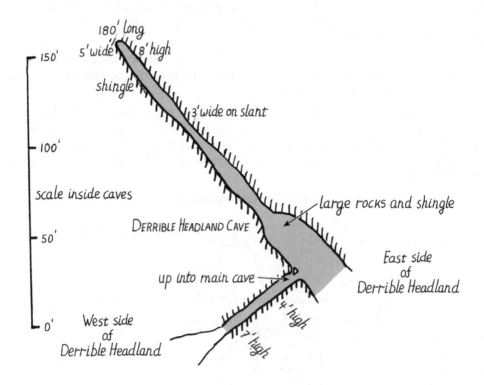

Starting from the beach below the col, a low cave (barely six feet high) leads under the headland. On the east side, this cave emerges into another, larger cave close to the larger cave's entrance. This cave runs back 180 feet into the larger part of the headland.

Leaving the south entrance on the east side, a CD+1.5m tide is required to scramble round to the south entrance of the Derrible Headland East Caves. The back of this cave is over two hundred and fifty feet from this entrance. About thirty feet into the entrance there is a pool that has to be waded to about knee deep. The cave curves round to the right and the roof lowers, and then it joins the main cave. For a good way into the cave from here, there is a ledge along the right wall. The ceiling is high and glistens in torch light in places. The back of the cave is round to the left, very thin and no light is visible from outside.

The way back to the main entrance is split by a floor to ceiling pillar. Twenty five feet before the entrance, an insignificant crack will be found on the left. This crack runs out passed the main entrance under an adjacent creek. The first part is narrow, and involves a traverse chimney style across a pool. At the end of this pool, it is possible to crawl between two boulders, one above and one below, and standing up to see light coming from above and ahead. However, the crack is too narrow to proceed any further.

Derrible Headland East Caves

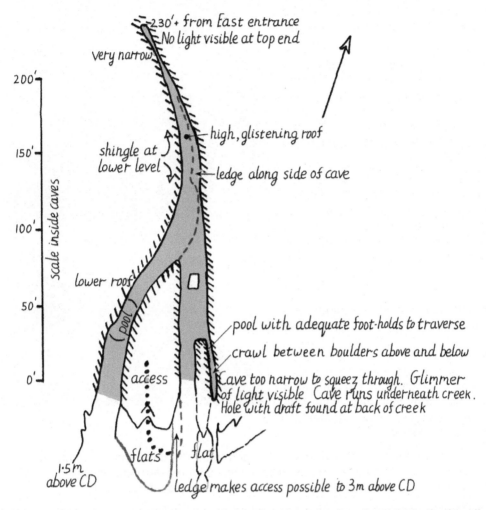

~230'+ from East entrance
No light visible at top end

very narrow

200'

high, glistening roof

shingle at lower level

ledge along side of cave

150'

scale inside caves

100'

lower roof

50'

(pool)

pool with adequate foot-holds to traverse

crawl between boulders above and below

0'

access

Cave too narrow to squeez through. Glimmer of light visible Cave runs underneath creek. Hole with draft found at back of creek

flats

flat

1·5m above CD

ledge makes access possible to 3m above CD

The main (East) entrance leads out to the creek with access on the right to the headland as described above. It is possible to climb up to the left and into the creek over the crack. A small hole can be found leading to the cave below: if there is no-one below to confirm that it is the right hole, the draft from below can be felt. There is another way up this side of the headland, reached by jumping across the creek towards the seaward end to gain the slab to the north, then round and up.

There is a cave running under Derrible headland from Petit Derrible. This cave, the Dungeon, is about one hundred and sixty five feet long, twelve feet wide and straight. It is possible to scramble round to petit Derrible from the East Caves: a tide of CD+1.2m is needed at the corner leading into Petit Derrible to avoid wading. Finally, there are two caves at the North end of Petit Derrible bay, one 24 feet long by 8 feet wide and one nearer l.w.s. 45 feet long.

Derrible Bay

Derrible is the East coast's sandy bay. The bay has the remarkable creux and the "L" cave which should more accurately be called the V cave.

The bay is not accessible over high water. People sometimes deliberately cut them selves off over high tide at neaps to (hopefully) have what is left of the bay to themselves, but check the previous high tide mark; spring tides come right up to the cliff all round.

The path down crosses a cave, not that you would notice. The flats at the bottom of the steps make a high tide swimming and picnic spot. To the right of the flats, the bottom is reached via a few slippery concrete steps. The cave to the right has a second exit.

From the bottom of the steps, you have to negotiate a rock and a boulder field to reach the shingle at the back of the bay or the sand. There is normally sand from above half tide down although the amount of sand, as in the other bays, is variable largely depending on the weather over the previous winter.

The little point between the extreme entrances to the "L" cave can be rounded at almost exactly half tide. The picture on the above shows the eastern entrances to the "L" cave with the top of the Derrible Creux behind. It was taken just above half tide.

The Derrible headland caves can be reached by scrambling and a short swim from the Bay: the final swim can be avoided by good climbers descending into the last creek. The Hog's Back cave to the West cannot be reach by scrambling, that is without a [long] swim.

Derrible Bay

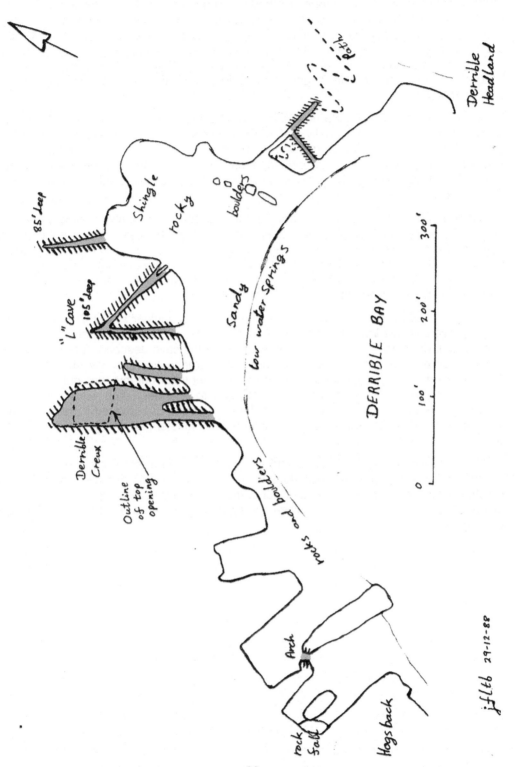

Shingle

rocky

boulders

85' Leap

"L" Cave

105' Leap

Sandy

low water Springs

Derrible Creux

Outline of top opening

rocks and boulders

Arch

rock fall

Hogs back

Path

Derrible Headland

DERRIBLE BAY

0   100'   200'   300'

jfLtb 29-12-88

Hog's Back Cave

The Dixcart entrance to the cave is reached by climbing down the East side of the creek, heading towards the cave. It will be necessary to go down almost to the bottom of the creek which requires a CD+2.3m tide. Climb up over the boulders towards the head of the creek, and the cave entrance is on the right. At this fall of tide, it is possible to get half way through the cave. You can go all the way through if you are prepared to swim the second half, some of it in limited light: a chest deep wade will be necessary at the best of times anyway.

Some, including the G & L Latrobe Guide, think that the cave is easier if entered from the Derrible entrance and it is virtually a stroll round the slabs from the Dixcart corner of the point. The rock is solid, the ledges wide and the odd, tiny climb easy. It is, however, a surprisingly long way. A final narrow ledge leads to this entrance, where there will be a shingle beach at CD+1m. The cave is only two feet wide at this point. At least entering from this end, the deepest wading is with what light there is behind you.

However, returning to the Dixcart entrance, the first part of the cave is straight for about sixty feet, although there is a two foot deep pool to paddle through. The cave then bends right and then left again and into another two foot deep pool. The far end of this pool is about half way through, in distance if not in excitement. There is a bouldery section, and a big boulder across the width which is now three or four feet: there is no light visible from outside along this section.

The sea level comes right up to the Derrible side of this boulder at CD+2m. If there are any significant waves here, the way out through the narrow Derrible entrance will be very difficult for swimmers. With a lower tide, the floor of the cave descends into a deep pool, which is believed to be between here and the entrance however low the tide drops. There is a ledge along the left hand (North) side underwater but this runs out as the cave curves round to the left and widens out to eight to ten feet. You will have to wade towards the entrance, chest deep. The bottom is smooth, but covered in seaweed. For some reason, there is always a giant shrimp/baby lobster/pair of eyes lurking in this pool...

The cave bends to the right again and the pool shallows before the narrow, Derrible entrance. The way round the rock slabs is on the right. So you can take this cave from whichever end you like, wading into or out of the dark! And aside from the cave, the end of the Hog's Back is a glorious place for swimming, scrambling, fishing or just sun bathing.

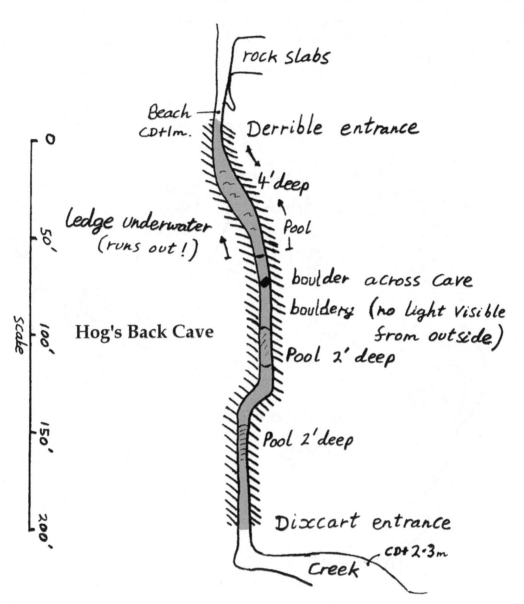

rock slabs

Beach CD+1m.

Derrible entrance

4' deep

Ledge underwater (runs out!)

Pool

boulder across cave

Hog's Back Cave

boulders (no light visible from outside)

Pool 2' deep

Pool 2' deep

Dixcart entrance

CD+2·3m

Creek

Scale

0
50'
100'
150'
200'

Dixcart Bay and Cave

Dixcart Bay has a natural arch under the rock spur at the middle of the back of the bay. There is a cave, almost an arch with a right angle, under the "Sugar Loaf", a large detached rock on the South West side of the bay. The bay is mostly pebbles but with course sand on the east side around the HW mark and a sand strip at very low tide mostly towards the west side.

Dixcart Bay Cave

This is the second longest cave in Sark and one of the most accessible. However for some reason, the air inside is rather smelly. The cave is on the left hand side of Dixcart Bay and the tide needs to be down to CD+2.7m to reach the entrance. The cave is about 315 feet long. There are four pools inside the cave to be negotiated, the second and third being thigh deep wades in murky water. The cave is quite narrow, down to four feet at times, and is completely dark from half way in.

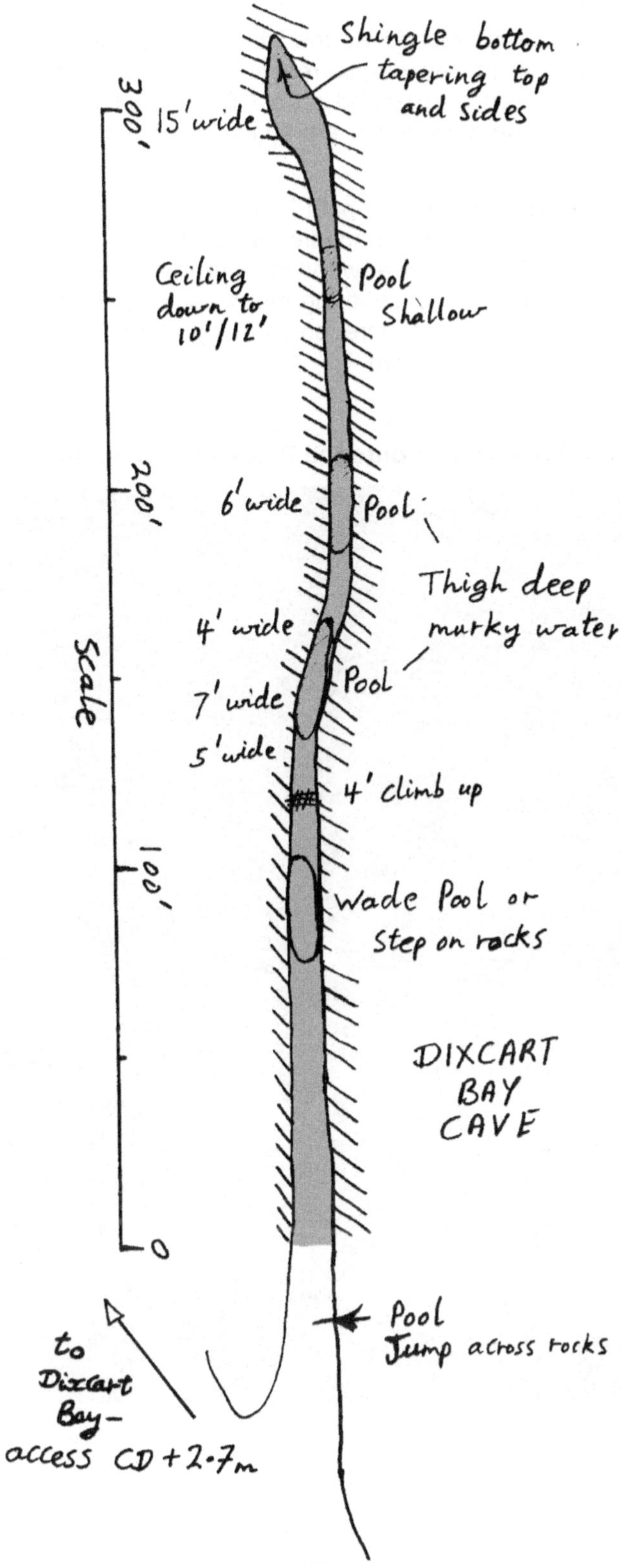

Shingle bottom
tapering top
and sides

15' wide

300'

Ceiling
down to
10'/12'

Pool
Shallow

200'

6' wide

Pool

Thigh deep
murky water

Scale

4' wide

Pool

7' wide

5' wide

4' climb up

100'

Wade Pool or
Step on rocks

DIXCART
BAY
CAVE

0

to
Dixcart
Bay —
access CD + 2·7m

Pool
Jump across rocks

43

Noir Bais to Pigeon Cave

All of this section of coast is reached via the Dixcart Souffleur flats. The Noir Bais, the southern most point of Dixcart Bay, can be reached on a CD+1m tide. The low, red cave before the Pigeon Cave can be reached on a CD+0.25m tide. The Pigeon Cave will always require a deep wade, unless you are an excellent climber or there is an unheard of CD-1m tide!

To find a way down, start along the cliff path from La Coupée towards Dixcart, and strike down from the right hand bend after a hundred yards or so. Cut down and round to the left, across a small dip. An alternative when coming from Dixcart is to turn down at the end of the sloe bushes after the second big dip in the path. Either way, a rocky ridge leads to a way down, and left some more, onto the top of the Dixcart Souffleur flats. The picture below shows the final way down.

Looking down onto the Dixcart Souffleur flats

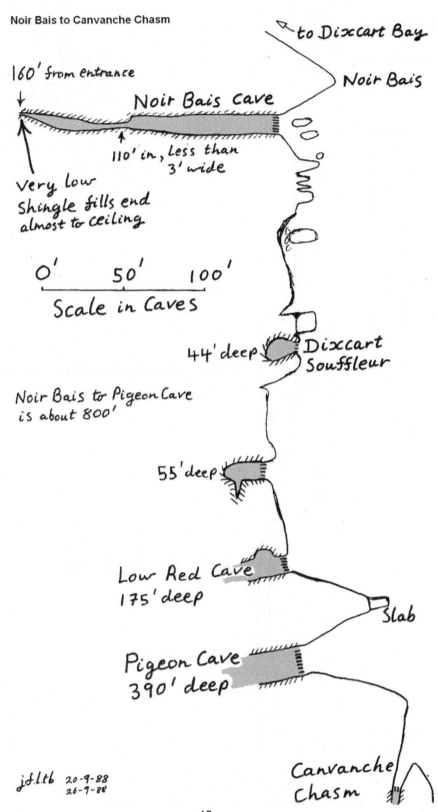

to Dixcart Bay

Noir Bais

160' from entrance

Noir Bais Cave

110' in, Less than 3' wide

Very low
Shingle fills end
almost to ceiling

0'   50'   100'

Scale in Caves

Noir Bais to Pigeon Cave
is about 800'

44' deep   Dixcart Souffleur

55' deep

Low Red Cave
175' deep

Slab

Pigeon Cave
390' deep

jf.ltb 20-9-88
        26-9-88

Canvanche
Chasm

45

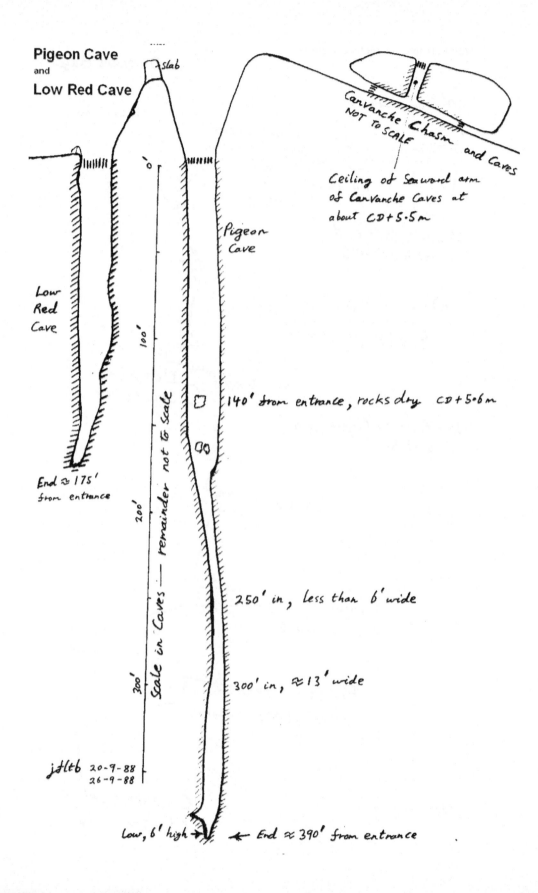

Pigeon Cave
and
Low Red Cave

slab

Canvanche Chasm and Caves
NOT TO SCALE

Ceiling of Seaward arm
of Canvanche Caves at
about CD+5.5m

0'

Pigeon
Cave

Low
Red
Cave

100'

140' from entrance, rocks dry   CD+5.6m

End ≈ 175'
from entrance

200'

Scale in Caves — remainder not to scale

250' in, less than 6' wide

300'

300' in, ≈ 13' wide

j h lt b   20-9-88
          26-9-88

Low, 6' high →   ← End ≈ 390' from entrance

There is a steep gully going down the back (north side) of the flats. However there is no shortage of foot and hand holds. The last three feet is an overhang, but there is a strategic boulder sticking up at the seaward end of the gully to provide a footing on the last drop. From the bottom, on shingle at this point, is a one hundred yard, bouldery scramble to the Noir Bais.

Just before the point, there is a cave on the left with a large rock pool in front of it. The cave is one hundred and sixty feet long. Two thirds of the way in it narrows to less than three feet wide, but it opens out again before the end. At the back of the cave, the shingle rises up almost to the ceiling, and there is insufficient space to be able to crawl to the very end.

Back at the Dixcart Souffleur flats, climbing down the gentler slope to the south, a CD+0.25m tide is needed to scramble into the Souffleur Cave. There is a dip in the shingle at the entrance and the resultant pool will have to be waded knee deep. The Souffleur Cave has a narrow entrance (about eight feet wide) and is about forty four feet from front to back. It is almost circular inside, about fifteen feet high and with the entrance only a very little lower than the roof.

Round the corner, there is a steep rock slope down from above the Souffleur which offers an alternative way down this side for the confident, able climber. From here to the low, red cave a CD+1m tide is adequate. On the way, a high, open cave fifty feed deep and with a side arm to the left is passed. The low, red cave is one hundred and seventy five feet long and mostly has a bare, undulating rock floor. It tapers from about twenty feet wide to six feet wide and six feet high.

Further progress to the Pigeon Cave is halted by vertical rock face running out to the end of the slab separating it from the low, red cave. The outer end of this slab is accessible at sea level from the Pigeon Cave without getting wet, but a wade chest deep is required on this side: the bottom is estimated at one meter below chart datum. For the accomplished climber, it is possible to climb up a crack which starts at the point the sea reaches at CD 0.25. There is a slight overhang to be negotiated, and the rocks are covered in an amount of marine growth. It is a gentle scramble down the slab on the other side.

The Pigeon is believed to be the longest natural cave in the island. It is possible to take a small boat in over a third of the way at high tide. Between two and three hundred feet in, the width is reduced to less than six feet on one section. The cave opens out to over twelve feet wide again before the back, which is over three hundred and ninety feet from the entrance. The back is only about six feet high, and there is a short side arm to the right.

Canvanche Chasm and Lamentation Caves

There is no safe way from the top of Sark down to the Canvanche Caves, the East side of La Coupée or the Lamentation Caves. There is an old route down across the top of the East entrance to the Canvanche Caves: one slip on a loose slope and you would end up in the Canvanche Chasm. So access will have to be scrambling and swimming ("coasteering") either from the Dixcart Souffleur or from the Pot, or by landing from a boat.

The Canvanche Caves have wonderful light when visited by boat: but there are tales of a boat being pushed against the ceiling by an unexpected swell in the side cave, the roof of which is about 5.5m above chart datum. They are no less spectacular on foot. An exceptionally low tide is needed for it to be possible to walk to the Eastern cave entrance: the tide is back to the T junction inside the cave at about CD+0.5m.

The Lamentation Caves

The Lamentation Caves are on the Little Sark side of the "steep side of La Coupée". The main caves form a T with the tail about 110 feet from the entrance to top, and the top about 100 feet long. The entrance on the East end of the top of the T points towards the south side of Baleine, about towards the middle of Balmée.

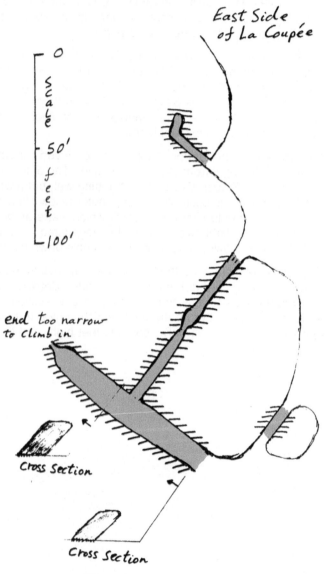

East Side of La Coupée

Scale of feet

0

50'

100'

end too narrow to climb in

Cross Section

Cross Section

48

Pot to Venus Pool

The final approach is a descent inside the Pot itself. There are now two exits to the sea, the larger towards the south and a narrower opening to the north. North from the Pot, a scramble leads to the Three Brothers rocks. Further progress to the Moie Fano ("Puffin Headland") requires a swim.

South from the Pot to the Sweet Pea Cave is a somewhat slippery scramble over seaweed covered boulders, many of which seem to have sharp, pointed tops! The Sweet Pea Cave is unusual in being near the high water mark. It has two entrances, is just under 140' long with a pool for nearly half of its length.

Sweet Pea Cave

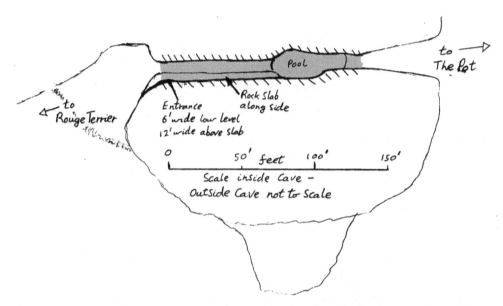

The South end of the Sweet Pea Cave leads down into a creek. The bottom at the far side of this creek is at about chart datum. It is possible to climb round at about, or a little above, the high water mark, starting from down in the creek at about CD+1.8m. This traverse leads eventually to Rouge Terrier. Half way between the Sweet Pea Cave and Rouge Terrier, it is easy to walk up to meet the path from La Cloture (the Barracks) to Rouge Terrier, but the worst of the traverse is over by then anyway.

At Rouge Terrier, you can climb down towards the South and gain the beach by Breniere (The Ladies Slipper). You can walk between Breniere and Sark, or through the cave in the shore-ward part of Breniere (about 60' long).

The scramble across the rocks round Clouet is relatively easy, with sections across rock slabs and dropping down into the occasional creek. There some old walls on the end of the promontory half way across Clouet which are reputed to be part of an old fortification.

In the South West corner of Clouet, there are two caves, both rather dank, smelly and slippery under foot. The more northerly, which runs in to the North West, is straight, about 150' long and between 6' and 15' wide, the width varying in and out up into the cave. The other is tucked away in the corner of the bay, behind a large rock which stands just clear of the island. This cave runs straight in to the South West at a constant width of about 8' for 75', and then bends to the left and narrows. The end, about 115' from the entrance, is almost pitch dark.

Venus Pool is at the South end of Clouet. This is much visited, and the way up and down is easy even if some find it difficult to locate the pool.

Caves in Clouet Bay

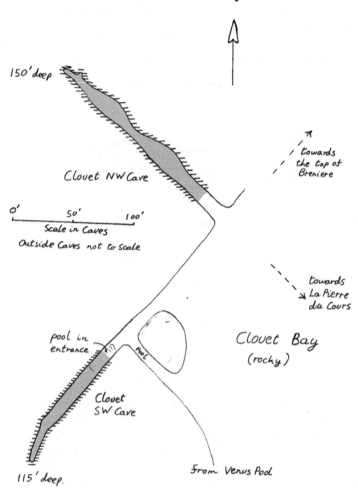

Venus Pool

The start of the way down to Venus Pool is between two cairns. The route starts to the left (heading towards the vertical drop to the side of Venus Pool) and then slopes down across the rock to the right.

Once down onto the rock slabs, Venus Pool is well round to the left. There is no mistaking it when you see it, with a vertical rock slab at the back. The pool is approached over the lowest corner overflowing into a creek, and this is the point to be watched on a rising tide. There is no safe way up from the East side of the pool.

Round to the right (West) of the way down and a gentle scramble, there are some sheltered spots with reasonably smooth (if not level) rock.

Venus Pool

Photo: Martina La Trobe Bateman

South Corner – Louge Creek

There is a creek shown on some maps as "Plat Rue Bay" to the West of the Venus Pool headland. This creek looks out into the gap between Sercul and Bretaigne Uset. On the West side of this creek is a small cave with an entrance about 10 feet wide and internally about 30 feet in diameter. Although not very large in cave terms, this is the Little Sark souffleur, spectacular with a swell and wind from the SW.

Scrambling from this cave to the West, there is a 125 foot long cave leading to the Louge creek. This cave narrows to three feet wide at the Eastern end. Not strictly narrow enough to be a "fat man's misery", it is reputed to be a tight squeeze in a canoe! When scrambling, there is a pool, starting about 15 feet from the eastern entrance and about 45 feet long, to be waded through.

Louge Creek

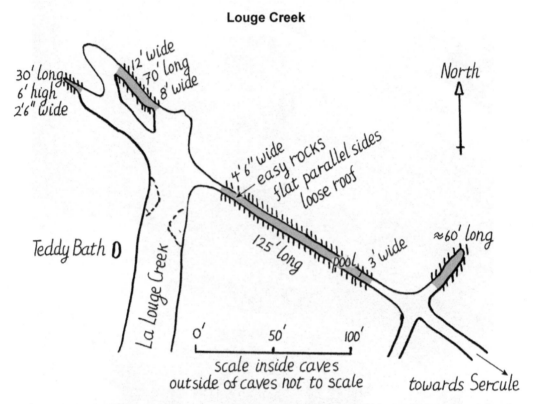

La Louge creek can be entered by boat: a small boat (e.g. 16' long, 6' beam) can enter from the sea, and turn first left into the creek with a small cave at the end. There is evidence of a raised beach above this cave.

The West side La Louge Creek towards the seaward end can be reached from the land although there is not a maintained path. This is good swimming and sunbathing place in clement weather. The top end of the creek can be reached dry at low water springs, or you can swim in. In the tradition of giving place names, there is a [small] pool in the flats called on some maps "Teddy Bath".

Sheep Smuggling?

James LTB, sheep loader

This is a true story, not just a shaggy sheep tail (sic). On a leisurely round the island trip in The Surprise, we went up into The Louge Creek, turning left at the top towards the end below the raised beach. On the rocks at the head of the creek (and no doubt grateful that is was not a spring tide!) was a sheep which had apparently fallen down the cliff. The sheep appeared undamaged, if not a little hungry.

Loading a sheep onto a 16' boat even in calm weather from the rocks at the end of the creek was not easy. However, the sheep was successfully loaded (see photo), but the question was "what next?" We decided to land the sheep at Port Gorey, which, after all, was near to home as far as the sheep was concerned.

Visitors viewed us suspiciously: Sark obviously has some very odd local customs!

Rouge Câne and Adonis

The path down Rouge Câne is not usually maintained and is more akin to a sheep track, but otherwise is not particularly difficult and there are some steps at the bottom. Rouge Câne is very rocky and the off lying sea is riddled with boat-trap rocks. The bay, if you can even call it that, is rugged and ethereal, a place for when the weather is rough!

Adonis Pool is in the rocks opposite La Moie de la Bretaigne ("Ship Rock"). Access is over the end of Adonis Headland, the trickiest part being crossing the gulley at the bottom.

Les Fontaines (Little Sark) to Grande Grève

Although there are no deep caves between Les Fontaines Little Sark and Grande Grève, this is another of the classic Sark low tide scrambles, and does include a real "Fat Man's Misery". The scramble can be attempted from either end.

Les Fontaines to Grand Grêve Scramble

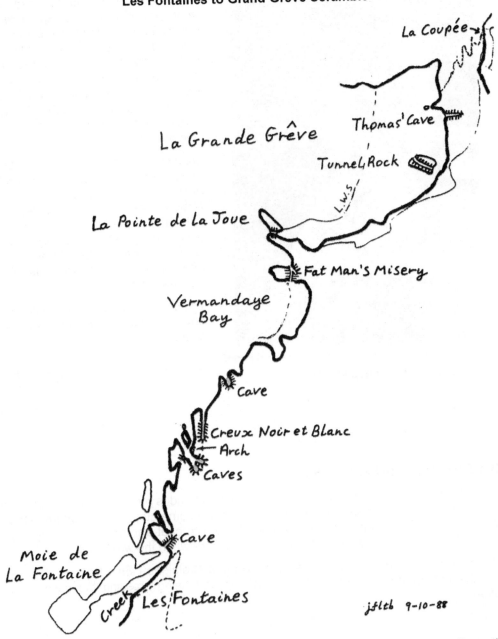

La Coupée

La Grande Grêve

Thomas' Cave

Tunnel Rock

La Pointe de la Jove

L.W.S.

Fat Man's Misery

Vermandaye Bay

Cave

Creux Noir et Blanc

Arch

Caves

Cave

Moie de La Fontaine

Creek Les Fontaines

jfltb 9-10-88

From Les Fontaines Little Sark, there is a small cave before the first corner. From this corner to Le Creux Noir et Blanc, there is a series of lovely little creeks, some with backs running parallel to the coast. Some of the faults can be traced from one creek to the next.

This scramble requires a tide down to CD+1m and even then there are some pools to be negotiated. Before Le Creux Noir et Blanc there is a short through cave: Le Creux Noir et Blanc itself is relatively uninteresting. Between Le Creux Noir et Blanc and La Vermandaye, there are a couple of small caves. One has an internal diameter of about 40 feet.

On the North side of La Vermandaye is the Fat Man's Misery. The cave is about 60 feet through, with the narrowest point about half way. Towards the North entrance, the exit is wider. The North entrance is not quite in line with the Southern part of the cave and extends back into a dead end.

Grande Grêve is reached via the cave through La Pointe de la Joue. Gaining access to the Southern entrance without wading may require a climb. However, the very brave may climb up on one side of the entrance, and jump across onto a ledge on the other. This ledge then leads through the cave towards the bay.

Grande Grêve

The path down from La Coupée gives access to the NE corner of the bay at all states of the tide. The SW part of the bay is accessible from half tide down. This part of the bay is cut off over the top half of the tide which reaches right up to the cliff edge at springs. The top of the beach is shingle, but much of the bay gives way to a large expanse of sand as the tide goes down, There is a patch were your feet sink into the sand behind an isolated rock beyond the tunnel rock. As in other bays, the amount of sand at the top of the bay is variable.

Thomas' Cave is immediately round the first outcrop into the bay when coming from the steps: this outcrop can be passed at about half tide. The cave is only 60 feet long, but the back is above water on most tides. The cave is named after Thomas who was lost in this cave for a whole high water when barely a toddler.

There is a grotto in the rocks at the back of the Southern part of the sandy part of the beach accessible only at low tide. The Tunnel Rock, in the middle of the bay, has a cave all the way through about 80 feet long, tapering from 5 or 6 feet wide at the sea entrance to 8 to 10 feet wide at the beach entrance.

Port ès Sais

The scramble from Grande Grêve to Port ès Sais is not possible without a swim. Port ès Sais is not normally accessible from the land, and the back is subject to frequent falls. From time to time, untrustworthy ropes are put down some sections.

The cave in the East corner of the bay has a man made tunnel starting above the bottom of the cave on the left hand side. This tunnel, made presumably in search of metal ore, is believed to lead under the Dos d'Ann, but has not been explored (unsafe?).

There are a couple of caves on the North and West side of the bay. One is about 185 feet long, ten to twelve feet wide at the entrance narrowing to eight feet wide. There are a couple of small caves towards the West, the first 15/20 feet long and the second 25/30 feet long. Just before the North Western corner of the bay is cave about 137 feet long, 5/6 feet wide with a pool in the entrance. This cave looks towards the tunnel rock in Grande Grêve which is just visible from the entrance to the right of the point between Grande Grêve and Port ès Sais. Round the corner is a drop of some 15 to 20 feet over a big bolder into a pool which leads inside the pinnacle rocks to the entrance of the Orgerie Caves.

Orgeries

The Moie des Orgeries has a great area of rock flats facing West. In stormy weather, the seas break right up them. In calmer times, it is possible to swim round to explore the creeks on either side and across to a cave system. Or just sun bathe.

Take the road from the Beauregard towards the Monument. The road makes a left turn (straight on leads to the Fregondée) and a right turn where it becomes a track. At this right turn, head straight on down the side of a field, now a vineyard, heading south. A gate leads onto an enclosed common area. Once through the gate, you must bear to the right (either side of a thicket), heading roughly towards the end of little Sark, making way down a little valley to the right. Sheep tracks lead through the prickles (with any luck) at the top of the cliffs to a neck of land joining on to the top of the Moie des Orgeries.

This neck is wide and not at all heady up to this point. The creeks on either side are joined by an archway, but this is not apparent from up here. The way to the rock slabs and the sea is straight down. You must pick your own route, but following the line of a fault towards the Havre Gosselin side is probably the easiest.

There is a cave system across the South Creek. It is only accessible by swimming across the creek from the Orgerie flats or by climbing round from Port ès Sais. The system has three sea entrances, and a series of caves inside all running in different directions. There are large pinnacle rocks, almost stacks outside the entrances to the caves.

Orgeries Caves

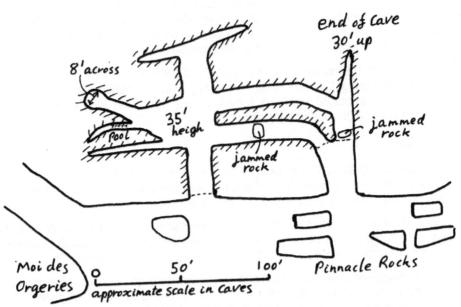

The outline on which the map above is based was drawn by RGS LTB.

The creek that separates the Moie des Orgeries from the island can be accessed without swimming from the South East corner of the Orgerie slabs on a tide down to CD+0.7m. Heading NW through the creek leads through a two foot deep pool under an arch which is about 50 foot long. The way down crossed over the top of this arch.

Pinnacle Rocks outside the Orgeries Caves

At the junction in this creek at the North corner of the Moie des Orgeries, the creek continues eventually terminating in a 50 foot long cave, 8 to 12 foot wide. On the NE of the junction, there is a narrow slot in the rocks 12 to 18 inches wide, a continuation of the wide, vertical sided creek from the sea. This can be accessed from above over a pool.

There are a number of other slots, some becoming caves, NW of here. Before the Victor Hugo cave is a souffleur which blows at low water springs.

The North side of the seaward entrance to the Victor Hugo Cave (not measured) can be reached from the headland below the Monument, but the entrance itself never dries out. This large cave has a high, domed ceiling and a second entrance/exit high up at the back. In calm weather - there is usually a swell here - it is possible to swim into the cave or to take a boat in.

Coast Orgeries to Victor Hugo

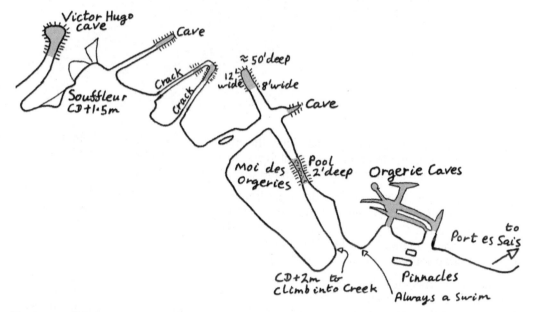

Fregondée

This is a little visited bay that never really has any decent sunlight.

Gouliot Caves

The Gouliot Caves are famous for the marine life clinging to their walls, particularly the sea anemones in different colours. Some part of the caves can be entered at any time, but a tide of CD+1.0m or lower is really needed for the inner passages.

Take the path from Beauregard to the Gouliot Headland: where a little valley gives way to the beginning of the headland, a path starting down on the right will be found. This leads down above a creek on the right with the Gouliot flats visible beyond. The path turns to the left and along the top of a sloping rock slab before arriving at the top entrance to the Gouliot Chimney, which is well above sea level. This cave is wide, high and drafty!

Northern Approach to Gouliot Caves

Climb down inside the Chimney which joins the main highway of the Gouliots, the Outer Passage. It can be fun to come here at high tide to watch the water rushing through both from the main south entrance and through the Sunny Pool opposite.

The Outer Passage is over two hundred feet from south to north exit. Heading north from the junction with the Chimney and the Sunny Pool, an opening will be found on the left which leads to the Octopus Pool. This offers a short cut to the inner passage - for the brave who are prepared to wade. The pool bottom slopes gently down, but at the far end it is chest deep with an almost vertical climb out.

It is the inner passages that are renown for the marine life. The usual way in is to walk out of the north entrance to the Outer Passage and follow the cliff edge round on the left. Two slits lead through to a shingle beach and the way to the Inner Passage is on the far side on the left. Crossing the head of this beach is where the tide is critical.

Gouliot Caves

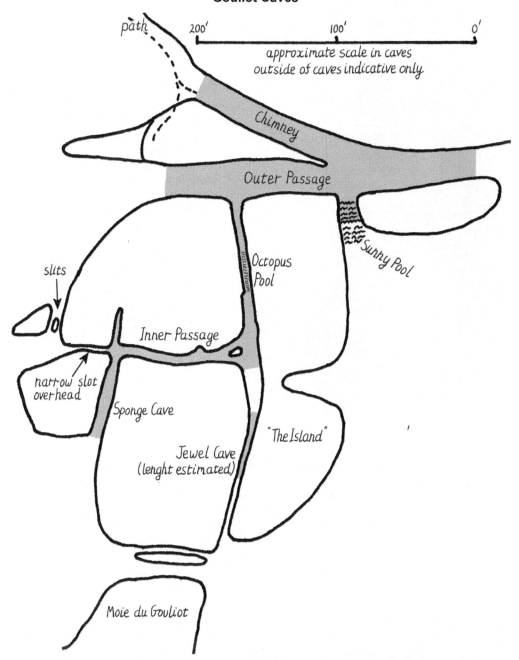

path   200'   100'   0'

approximate scale in caves
outside of caves indicative only

Chimney

Outer Passage

Octopus
Pool

Sunny Pool

slits

Inner Passage

narrow slot
overhead

Sponge Cave

Jewel Cave
(lenght estimated)

"The Island"

Moie du Gouliot

The first part of the Inner Passage has a slot in the roof, and the cave proper starts at the junction with the Sponge Cave on the right which leads sixty five feet out to the sea.

Although called the Sponge Cave, sponges are more prolific elsewhere in the system. The way into the cave is low (about four feet high), but it opens out inside. There is also a thirty foot extension of the Sponge Cave on the left which has an even lower entrance, but which rises to just standing headroom at one place inside.

The picture on the left is inside the Gouliot Inner Passage, looking North. The Entrance to the Sponge Cave is on the left, opposite Mary LTB

The Inner Passage continues in gentle curves which prevent it being possible to see from one end to the other. There is nearly always a pool to wade through (see picture), but it is rarely more than knee deep. Along the way, there is a widening on the left and this dark location is a favourite with the white anemones. After passing either side of a central pillar, the Inner Passage joins the cave of the Octopus Pool, and looking right the way to the Jewel Cave is seen. There is a large opening up to the outside world and the "Island" (q.v.). The tide never retreats enough to be able to walk into Jewel Cave: a swim is always necessary.

South side of Gouliot Headland and Moie de Gouliot

Port à la Jument

Port à la Jument bay is accessed via a path starting from a track past Le Port Farm and the entrance to The Petit Champ Hotel. The top of the path can also be reached from the côtil above the Gouliot Headland, passing optionally the top of the Saut à Juan, then the Gouliot survey point (see page 72) and following the field boundary on your left. Below the survey point, there is a quarry and it is possible to climb with care down to the sea to a place known by some as "**The Home of the Gull**". The main entrance to the Moie de Mouton cave can be seen from these flats, but the cave cannot be reached without a reasonable swim.

The GSGS4 map shows the path through Le Port farm itself but the path has been diverted below the house in the intervening years. Jument gives access to the back entrance to the Moie de Mouton cave. The bay is mostly rocky. However there are excellent sunbathing places at the bottom of the path and is good for high tide swimming. The northern part of the bay has a small patch of sand at a very low tide.

North Port à la Jument bay looking towards Tintageu at LWS

Moie de Mouton Cave

The Moie de Mouton is at the WSW corner of La Port à la Jument and this cave runs through it. The two ends of the cave are quite different. The distance underground between the entrances, round the corners is about three hundred and ninety feet. The maximum distance between entrances in the Boutiques is under two hundred and ninety feet (north entrance to first hall). The Pigeon Cave is believed to be the longest natural cave round Sark and it is the same length, all-be-it that it has only one entrance and runs straight in.

This cave is a favourite with round the island boat trips which can enter the main entrance in calm weather. Spectacular as this can be, there is much more to the cave. The cave can be accessed on a CD+1.8m tide with a scramble from the bay and a short climb with good hand-holds.

From the bottom of the path down into the bay from Le Port farm, head across to the west round the base of the Moie. Scramble over the rocks, climb up onto the slabs at the seaward end of the bay and work round to a creek with a cave entrance on the left. Near the head of the creek is a place where it is possible to climb down. A tide of CD+1.8m is required at the bottom.

The drop is about ten feet. There are good hand-holds, especially at the top and the climb is not as bad as it looks from the top. However, every individual must make up their own mind about whether or not to tackle the climb. On an exceptionally low tide, it is possible to walk round the end of the creek: otherwise the safe way in is to wade.

This is really the back entrance to the cave. It runs in for about fifty feet, before turning to the right. Standing up just round the corner, it is just possible to see light at a higher level coming from the other end. This part of the cave gets lower, down to about three foot, after which there is usually a shallow pool. A hole leading to the upper level can now be seen above, but it is too small to climb into. The way continues through a pool, which can be over knee deep, but it leads to a long slot at the end of which is a step up into the upper level. Even when the rest of the cave appears calm, a draft fairly whistles through here.

Thirty feet back is the end of the upper part of the cave for humans, although a narrow slot can be seen running back towards the way in.. From here it is three hundred feet to the main entrance. For the first hundred feet, the walls, floor and ceiling are smooth and rounded. Although the cave is about fourteen feet wide at the step up from the lower level, much of this end of the cave is only six feet or so wide. There is a slight right hand kink in the cave, and the full width and height of the main entrance can be seen.

The front of the cave has smooth, mostly flat walls and a flat ceiling: the walls and ceiling meet at right angles. The front of the cave is generally about twelve feet wide, but projections and ledges from the sides restrict this to about nine feet in places. Also of interest to boats entering the cave, once the rocks forty feet into the cave have been crossed, there are no rocks higher for the next hundred feet. You can walk out of the main entrance to the cave, but not out of the creek.

Moie de Mouton Cave

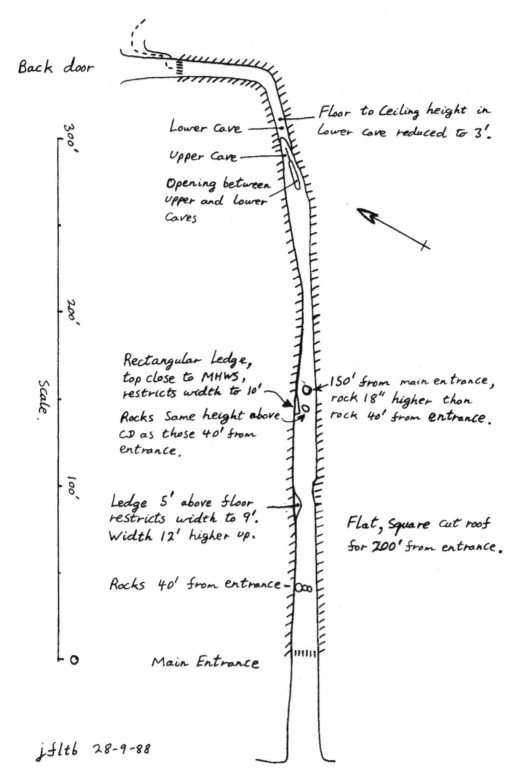

Back door

Floor to Ceiling height in lower cave reduced to 3'.

Lower Cave

Upper Cave

Opening between upper and lower Caves

300'

200'

Scale.

Rectangular ledge, top close to MHWS, restricts width to 10'.

Rocks Same height above CD as those 40' from entrance.

150' from main entrance, rock 18" higher than rock 40' from entrance.

100'

Ledge 5' above floor restricts width to 9'. Width 12' higher up.

Flat, Square cut roof for 200' from entrance.

Rocks 40' from entrance

0

Main Entrance

jfltb 28-9-88

Pegâne

Pegâne, between Port à la Jument and Port du Moulin, is interesting not because of any long caves, but because there is a fault running parallel to the back of the bay that can be followed across the back of a number of creeks and small caves. Pegâne can be reached on any low tide from Port du Moulin heading south passed the end of Tintageu. There is a low tide scramble form Port à la Jument but a good spring tide is required at the North side of Port à la Jument.

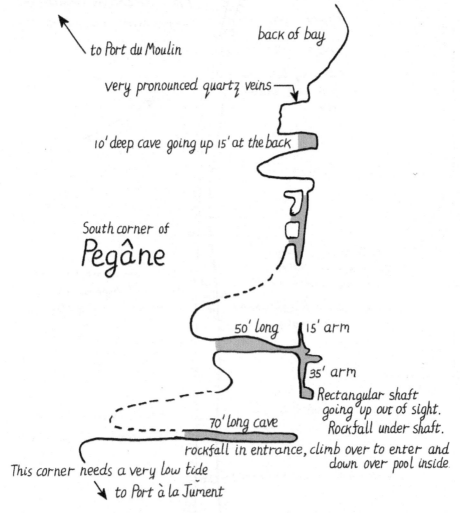

to Port du Moulin

back of bay

very pronounced quartz veins

10' deep cave going up 15' at the back

South corner of

Pegâne

50' long

15' arm

35' arm

Rectangular shaft going up out of sight. Rockfall under shaft.

70' long cave

rockfall in entrance, climb over to enter and down over pool inside.

This corner needs a very low tide

to Port à la Jument

There is a 70' foot long cave at the south extremity of the bay. The next cave goes in a mere 50 feet, and then branches both left and right. The right branch is about 35 feet long, at the end of which is a high man made rectangular shaft going up. Apparently some semi precious stone used to be mined here. The fault forming the branches at the back of this cave can be traced through the backs of three other small caves and the back of the creeks in the bay.

Port du Moulin

Port du Moulin is a shingle beach giving way to larger but smooth stones below about half tide. Despite this, this bay is a good afternoon swimming place or for a beach barbecue. Although the tide comes to the top of the beach all along at high water springs, the top of the beach is accessible at most tides, and particularly at neaps (high water around lunch time).

A gap through to the south leads via a simple scramble to Pegâne, accessible from half tide down. The arch at the North end of the bay is also passable from half tide down and leads to Saignie bay and the Seven Dimples.

Port du Moulin looking towards Le Bec du Nez

Photo: Martina La Trobe Bateman

The picture above was taken at low water springs looking over the Port du Moulin Arch and Les Autelets, on beyond the Seven Dimples to the Bec.

The Seven Dimples

The Seven Dimples is another of Sark's classic low tide scrambles, requiring a tide down to CD+0.6m at the North end of Saignie Bay. Whilst the scramble itself is from Saigne to Le Platon, one must start from Port du Moulin.

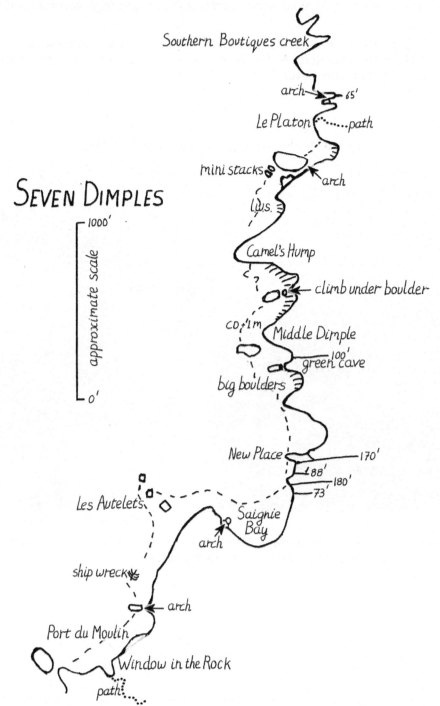

Southern Boutiques creek

arch — 65'

Le Platon ·······path

mini stacks

arch

l.u.s.

Seven Dimples

1000'

approximate scale

Camel's Hump

climb under boulder

co. 1m   Middle Dimple

100'
green cave

big boulders

0'

New Place — 170'

88'
180'
73'

Les Autelets

Saignie Bay

arch

ship wreck

arch

Port du Moulin

Window in the Rock

path

At the North end of Port du Moulin, proceed through the arch. Just around the corner is a pair of creeks joined at the back which at some time was a pair of caves joined at the back. There is a scramble over large rocks to Saignie Bay, towards Les Autelets (the Altar Rocks). On the way amongst the rocks nearer the low tide mark will be found the ribs of a ship wrecked for a film started but never finished made between WW I and WW II.

The South side of Saignie has a very large rock arch, almost a curved cave. At the top of a spring (that is necessarily at about 8:00 o'clock), it is possible to take a small boat through this arch. At low tide, it has a shingle or rocky bottom in common with all of Sagnie.

At the North East corner of Saignie, there are four caves under "The New Place". There was historically a way down for the brave from the Island at the New Place but has not been used for decades and is not now accessible.

Caves under The New Place

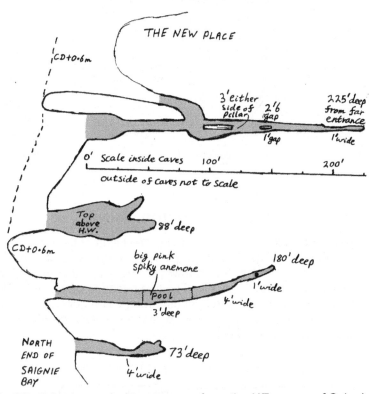

A tide down to CD+0.6m is needed to progress from the NE corner of Saignie beyond the entrance to the second cave round the corner to the third and fourth. The second and fourth caves are 180 and 170 feet long respectively. The fourth has two entrances, and the back of the cave is 225 feet in from the Southern most of these. This last cave also has pillars in the middle of the cave, and is only a foot wide in places toward the back.

The scramble crosses another inlet and the going requires negotiating larger boulders leading up to the Middle Dimple. To the South of the Middle Dimple, there is a cave which is quite green inside, if only 100 feet long.

The Middle Dimple is about half way in distance from Saignie to Le Platon flats. The scramble northwards passes the Camels Hump which gives an escape route to the Island. North of the Camel's Hump, the scramble leads past some little stacks, a rock on the island side looking like a wolf, and though an arch to a little rocky bay immediately south of Le Platon.

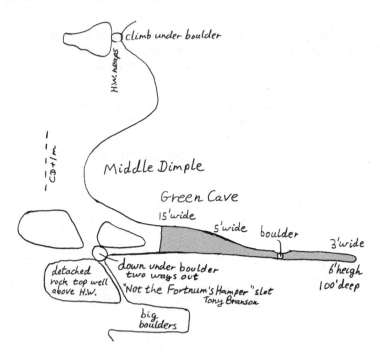

Le Platon

Le Platon is easily accessible via a path from the West side of the Eperquerie. Whilst this is the end (or beginning) of the Seven Dimples, Le Platon is at its best as a high tide afternoon place to swim from the flats. However, there are a couple of creeks with an arch and a cave immediately to the north. The tide needs to be down to CD+1.5 to climb dry into the creek to the north. An arch leads through to a second creek at the back of which is a 65' cave. The ceiling is too low to reach the back of this cave which has a small opening above near the entrance.

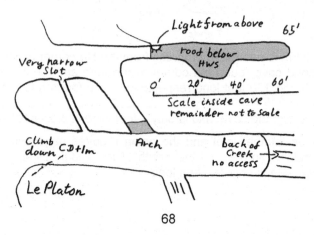

Boutiques

The Boutiques Caves under the west side of the Eperquerie allow you to exit four hundred and fifty feet from your entrance. Along the way, there are exits to the sea and side caves. It is possible to go through these caves at virtually any low water, and certainly on any early afternoon low water.

The easiest way is to start at the North end and work South through the caves. Walk north along the path on the Eperquerie, keeping to the right hand side approaching the Le Pertu separating the mainland of Sark from La Grune, the first of the off-lying islets. Follow round the end, turning to the left and getting progressively lower until you arrive on the flats on the west side of the north end. There is a convenient sloping ledge to reach the bottom of the inlet at the far side of which is the creek leading to the caves. There are two large boulders to pass: opinion is divided on the easiest side to pass the first (the author favours the right), but the second is passed on the left hand side of the creek.

Inside the The Boutiques
Looking out towards the Northern entrance

The entrance to the cave is about ten feet wide and about the same height. The going is easy under foot, mostly shingle to start with although there is sometimes a pool near the entrance. After a while, the cave tapers down to about six feet wide. Before the first opening to the sea on the right (the first Hall) after about two hundred and thirty five feet, there is nearly always a pool but this can usually be crossed by using the ledges at the side and a few judiciously placed boulders.

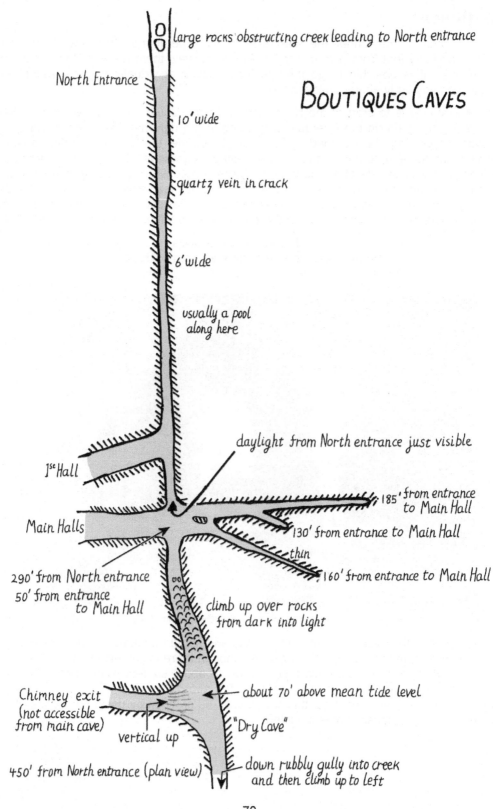

large rocks obstructing creek leading to North entrance

North Entrance

BOUTIQUES CAVES

10' wide

quartz vein in crack

6' wide

usually a pool
along here

daylight from North entrance just visible

1ˢᵗ Hall

185' from entrance
to Main Hall

Main Halls

130' from entrance to Main Hall

thin

290' from North entrance
50' from entrance
    to Main Hall

160' from entrance to Main Hall

climb up over rocks
from dark into light

Chimney exit
(not accessible
from main cave)

vertical up

about 70' above mean tide level

"Dry Cave"

450' from North entrance (plan view)

down rubbly gully into creek
and then climb up to left

The next sea entrance, the main hall, is a major junction. To the left are two caves running away from the sea which warrant a deviation from the main passage at this point. The back of the first is one hundred and thirty feet from the junction. There is a low rock to climb over just passed a small second opening into the other cave, and also a side arm off this cave about half way up. The second cave runs just over one hundred feet from the junction. Its floor is smoother, but it is quite narrow towards the top.

South from here, the character of the cave changes. The continuation of the cave from the junction is through a dark crack, and after a short distance light will be seen coming from in front and high up. There is now a climb up inside the cave over large boulders. There are occasional falls inside the cave which alter the difficulty on this climb. This climb is the main reason for starting at the north end as it is much easier to climb up into the light than down out of it.

At the top, in the Dry Cave, the exit will be seen ahead and is reached keeping to the left hand side. Down on the right is another exit to the sea the approach to which is loose rubble down a slope and there is a vertical drop at the end: it is dangerous to attempt to leave this way!

The southern exit is high above sea level. The way out is down the rubbly gully until it meets a gully from the sea to the top, and then back up to the left.

Gully leading to Southern entrance to the Boutiques Caves

Survey Points

A map of Sark, GSGS4, was made by the Survey Regiment of the Royal Engineers in 1964. Aerial photographs were taken by the Royal Air Force flying a Canberra on 27 April that year. To tie in the aerial photographs to the survey on the ground, six survey points were set up and marked on the day of the flight by crosses laid on the ground using white calico. The wooden stakes that marked these points have long since disappeared but these were the locations.

These six points were positioned around the coast so that each point could see one on either side.

Eperquerie

On the raised ground marked by a spot height of 203' just south east of the gun looking towards the butts. This is now overgrown.

Banquette

At the bottom of the field NE of Le Fort Farm. The hedges and trees particularly looking NW have grown up considerably in the intervening years, and you will have to move around now to see both sight lines.

Point Robert

This position is on private property. It is on the raised ground to the south of the top of the steps leading down to the lighthouse. However, you can see to the Banquette from the top of the lighthouse steps, and to Derrible on the track between La Valette and the Lighthouse.

Derrible

On the raised ground to the east of the Derrible dew pond, marked as a spot height 305'.

Little Sark Fort

This fort is on the highest point of Little Sark, spot height 330'. The site is now very overgrown with viscously prickly bushes. However, close examination will reveal a rectangle with a ditch and raised lip.

Gouliot

This is to the north of the track leading to the Gouliot headland, on the high point to the east of the Saut à Juan. From here, you can see north to the Eperquerie and, although it is not obvious, over the top of the track to the Monument back to the Little Sark fort.

This point is found by following the track from Beauregard towards the Gouliot Headland. At the field gate that gives onto the beginning of the côtil, turn right up the slope near to the field bank until passing through a gap in a bank. The cross was laid out just to the left (west).

Aerial Survey Reference Points

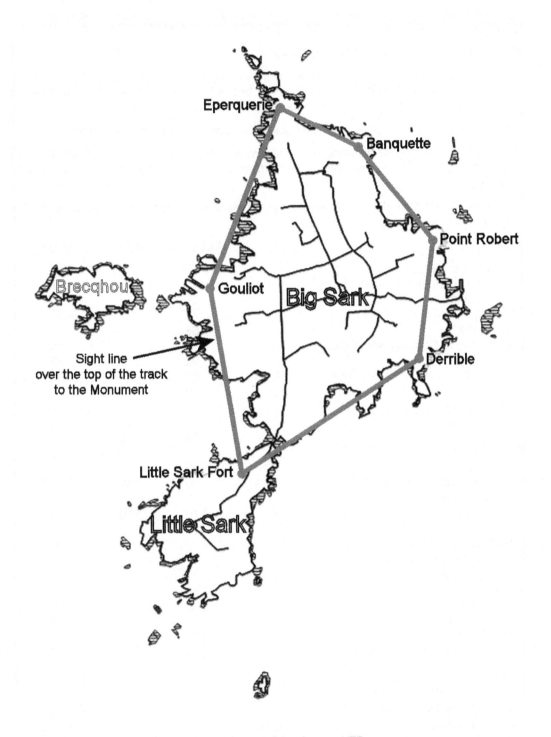

Digital outline of Sark on this page and page 6 by James LTB

An Inventory of Sark's Caves

The list below gives some details of significant Sark caves. However, there are many caves which are not listed below, and no doubt some are significant.

Cave names *in italics* are not in general use.

Distances are given in feet. The caves were mostly measured using a 300 foot fishing line, marked every 50 feet. The distances in between were estimated with outstretched arms. Overall, the accuracy on cave lengths is estimated at +/-5 feet plus +/-5%.

The "Length" (depth) given is from the back of the cave to the nearest entrance.

The "Run" is the longest distance between two entrances by the shortest route between them through the caves, *or the distance from the back of the cave to the farthest entrance.*

The assessment of angles and (particularly) curves in the caves has proved difficult. The angles in the sketches are all estimates.

Cave		Length	Run	Page
Fairy Arch, Twin Sisters [5]				*17*
Fern Cave (Les Fontaines)				*17*
Creux Belêt		88		*18*
unnamed [6]		75		*19*
unnamed [7]		68		*19*
Red Cave or Drinking Horse Cave		115		*19*
Huitriere		95		*19*
Banquette Caves or Blanc Caves,	*North*	88		
	South	80		*20*
Seven Caves				*22*
Gull's Chapel			35	*22*
2nd *Cave*		38	75	*22*
Dragon's Teeth			67	*22*
4th *Cave*		80		*24*
In and Out		80	150	*24*
Lighthouse Creux		110		*25*
Dog Cave		210	175 [8]	*26*
Maseline Halls		130	135	*30*
southern extension [9]			62	*30*
Maseline Gulls Chapel				*30*
Cagnon Cave				*31*
The Crypt		270		*32*
Cathedral Cave		200		*32*
Brown Cave		115		*34*
The Dungeon		165		*37*
Derrible Headland, East Caves		230	255 [10]	*37*

---

[5] arch at North end of Les Fontaines

[6] East of Red Cave

[7] East of Red Cave

[8] run measured from main entrance to exit via "The tail of the Dog".

[9] cave in line with main Maseline Caves Hall, but to the South.

[10] depth from back of cave to furthest sea entrance.

[11] one arm of this cave runs through Derrible Headland

[12] small cave between "L" cave and Derrible Creux.

[13] immediately East of Derrible entrance to Hog's Back Cave

[14] 2nd longest cave in Sark

[15] low red cave North of Pigeon cave

[16] longest cave in Sark

[17] East of Louge "Fat Man's Misery"

[18] leads to La Louge creek

[19] North side of La Vermondaye

[20] Grande Grêve

Feet to Metres

feet	metres	feet	metres	feet	metres		
'	m	'	m	'	m		
1	0.30	10	3.0	100	30		
2	0.61	20	6.1	200	61		
3	0.91	30	9.1	300	91		
4	1.22	40	12.2	390	119	Pigeon cave	
5	1.52	50	15.2	1000	305		
6	1.83	60	18.3				
7	2.13	70	21.3	inches	cms		
8	2.44	80	24.4	6	15		
9	2.74	90	27.4	12	30		
10	3.05	100	30.5	18	46		

---

[21] measured from the high, Northern entrance to the Southern entrance to the Outer Passage.

[22] measured from the true beginning of the cave at the junction with the Sponge Cave to the far (South) side of the common entrance with the Octopus Pool cave

[23] measured from junction with Outer Passage to the common entrance with the Inner Passage.

[24] from the junction with the inner passage to the seaward exit. The extension of the Sponge Cave back across the Inner Passage is about a further 30'.

[25] depth from back of cave to furthest sea entrance.

[26] just South of the Middle Dimple

Lightning Source UK Ltd.
Milton Keynes UK
UKOW05f2138150318

319529UK00005B/292/P